THE PENGUIN BOOK OF ENGLISH MADRIGALS

DENIS STEVENS

Q33

Denis Stevens, founder-conductor of the Ambrosian Consort and the Academia Monteverdiana, was educated at Oxford, London, and Paris – combining interests in languages, musicology, and chamber music. He specialized in medieval, Renaissance, and baroque programmes during his five years as a producer in the B.B.C. Music Division, which he left in 1954 for his first visiting professorship in America. After fulfilling invitations to Cornell, Columbia, California (Berkeley), and Pennsylvania State, he became a permanent member of the Department of Music at Columbia University in the City of New York. Dividing his time between research, teaching, and performance, he has made many gramophone records and festival appearances with his musicians, besides editing early music and publishing books such as *A History of Song*, *Tudor Church Music*, *Thomas Tomkins*, and (with Alec Robertson) *The Pelican History of Music*.

THE PENGUIN BOOK OF

English Madrigals

FOR FOUR VOICES

EDITED BY
DENIS STEVENS

PENGUIN BOOKS

Penguin Books Ltd, Harmondsworth, Middlesex, England
Penguin Books Inc., 3300 Clipper Mill Road, Baltimore, Md 21211, U.S.A.
Penguin Books Australia Ltd, Ringwood, Victoria, Australia

First published 1967

Printed in the United States of America

CONTENTS

Editorial Principles 7

BATESON

Down from above 13
If Love be blind 17
Phyllis, farewell 22
Whither so fast 25

BENNETT

O sleep, fond fancy 29
Weep, O mine eyes 34
Ye restless thoughts 37

BYRD

This sweet and merry month 42

FARMER

A little pretty bonny lass 50
Fair Phyllis 54
Take time 58

FARNABY

Ay me, poor heart 65
Construe my meaning 70
Some time she would 74
The curtain drawn 79

MORLEY

April is in my mistress' face 83
Die now, my heart 86
Now is the gentle season; In fields abroad 93
Say, gentle nymphs 100

MUNDY

My prime of youth; 105

PILKINGTON

Amyntas with his Phyllis fair 114
Have I found her? 119
Palaemon and his Sylvia 124
What though her frowns 129
Why should I grieve? 134

WILBYE

Adieu, sweet Amaryllis 139
As matchless beauty 143
Lady, when I behold 149
Thus saith my Cloris bright 154

FOR

ALEC ROBERTSON

on his seventy-fifth birthday

EDITORIAL PRINCIPLES

. . . and likewise you shall be perfectly understood of the auditor what you sing, which is one of the highest degrees of praise which a musician in dittying can attain unto or wish for. (Thomas Morley)

A choral group, perhaps, consisting mainly of amateur singers devoted to the madrigal and to comparable vocal forms and styles; or a group of soloists, working together towards great perfection but little reward, other than a purely musical one – no matter what way we hear madrigals performed, the most impressive, delightful, and memorable interpretations are those which breathe spontaneity of a completely natural and unaffected kind. As in so many musics, the art of madrigal singing thrives upon the concealment of art, so that very often the most natural and convincing effects derive from some hidden artifice, whose secret resides in experience, learning, intuition, or an amalgam of all three.

Given a generous allowance of years, experience emerges from practical pursuits, and learning from theoretical; but intuition, born of itself, cannot be commanded to appear, and it is the one ingredient of a fine performance that defies analysis and disarms criticism. Yet there is so much to be absorbed at the lower levels of technical accomplishment that it seems only right, in a brief exposition of editorial methods, to lay more stress upon matters lying nearly within our grasp; and it can hardly be denied that the most useful pre-requisite for a vital re-creation of early music is a text at one and the same time reliable and imaginative.

Music printers in sixteenth-century England were not always reliable, and even when proofs were corrected by unusually careful and conscientious composers, the possibility of error could not be entirely ruled out. But if the great majority of printed madrigals make good musical sense most of the time, the artistic sensibility characteristic of the finest underlay of text to music frequently leaves much to be longed for. Composers relied upon singers to adjust syllables to notes in a manner satisfactory to all concerned. Four hundred years ago, singers were used to such things, just as they were used to part-books bearing only isolated strands of a polyphonic web. Modern singers need scores; and they also need guidance in the matter of text underlay if the original source is at all doubtful or corrupt. These and related topics now call for our attention.

The individual vocal ranges of some Elizabethan madrigals pre-suppose a compass of enviable elasticity resulting perhaps from such social forms of encouragement described in Claude Hollybande's *The French Schoolemaister,* published in 1573:

'Roland, shall we have a song?'

'Yea Sir: where be your books of music? for they be the best corrected.'

'They be in my chest: Katherin, take the key of my closet – you shall find them in a little till at the left hand: behold, there be fair songs at four parts.'

'Who shall sing with me?'

'You shall have company enough: David shall make the bass, John the tenor, and James the treble.'

'Begin! James, take your tune! Go to: for what do you tarry?'

'I have but a rest.'

'Roland, drink afore you begin, you will sing with a better courage.'

'It is well said: give me some white wine – that will cause me to sing better.'

'You must drink some green wine!'

'Yea, truly, to cause me to lose my voice.'

'Oh, see what a funnel, for he hath poured a quart of wine without any taking of his breath.'

Notice that the treble or soprano part is taken not by the lady of the house but by James, probably a choirboy; notice too that the wine-bibber, Roland, is the alto or counter-tenor of this group. By the simple and simultaneous act of whetting his courage and wetting his whistle, he is ready to tackle those low D's more suited to a tenor, or those high E's within the province of a treble.

In the present selection of madrigals, extremes of tessitura have been purposely avoided, so that a normal vocal quartet can be assured of the following ranges:

Ex. 1

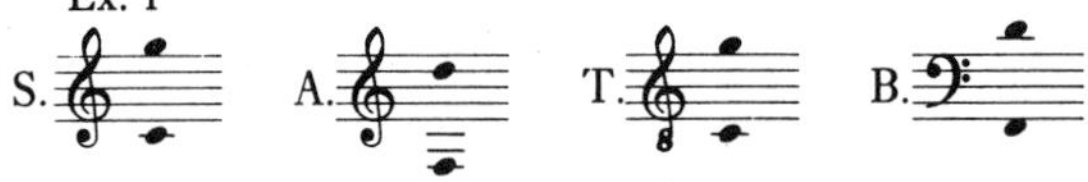

It would have been possible to include other works by subjecting them to transposition, but the very sight of a madrigal in the key of B flat minor or F sharp major has been known to strike cheerless chill in the hearts of even the doughtiest singers. Later volumes in this series may experiment along these lines, keeping within the bounds of two flats or two sharps in the key-signature; but for the present purposes non-transposition and medium range have been the guiding principles, and will help to avoid very low notes and very high ones, which Thomas Morley likened respectively to 'a kind of humming' and 'a constrained shrieking'. In some instances, uncomfortable ranges may be avoided by exchanging parts, but the result inevitably alters the tonal balance and has consequently been used in only one madrigal, Byrd's *This sweet and merry month,* a gem that we could ill afford to lose.

Tonality is such an outstanding characteristic of the madrigalian repertoire that it seems both logical and practical to employ modern key-signatures. Bateson's *Down from above* appears in the original part-books with no key-signature, but the profusion of F sharps and the frequent as well as final cadencing on G tell us that the simplest solution to the problem is the use of a G major key-signature. Bennett's *O sleep, fond fancy,* is just as clearly in G minor, and so the old signature of one flat has been replaced (with, of course, the necessary internal adjustments) by the modern key-signature of two flats. This principle has been followed throughout the volume, except in a rare instance of quasi-modality – Morley's exquisite pair of madrigals *Now is the gentle season* and *The fields abroad.*

One particular feature of the original part-books has been deliberately and consistently heeded, and that is the exclusion of tempo and dynamic markings. Freshness and spontaneity in performance are sometimes due to a feeling among the singers that they have made a personal contribution to the latent expressive powers of the music, and it is good that they or their director should be able to mould an interpretation after their own ideas, rather than slavishly follow the dynamic droppings of some pedantic editor. One recalls the school hymn written by the Headmaster and set to music by Dr Jolly in Aldous Huxley's *Antic Hay:*

(f) For slack hands and *(dim.)* idle minds
(mf) Mischief still the Tempter finds.
(ff) Keep him captive in his lair;
(f) Work will bind him. *(dim.)* Work is *(pp)* prayer.

Terrace-dynamics of this kind militate against the splendid subtleties of the madrigal and clamp its emotional promise in the strait-jacket of unimaginative reproduction. Let the artists decide for themselves how fast or how slow, how loud or how soft they intend to sing; but let them do so after reading the poem, which is printed here in full before the music begins.

There is, alas, one persuasive and all-pervading characteristic of the part-books that cannot be reproduced – the uninhibited free flow of notes and text without bar lines of any kind. As soon as polyphony is put into score, bar-lines become essential for modern singers and directors, and have in fact been used since the time of the earliest Renaissance scores. Although it is worth remembering that medieval scores disdained bar-lines, relying on rough-and-ready alignment combined with mensural practice to convince singers of their efficacy, a return to this ideal seems out of the question. If modern bar-lines provide welcome orientation, they do so because of their reliability and regularity. Cross-rhythms inherent in the music should not be permitted to dictate fancy barring, except when the shift in stress applies to all voice-parts.

Accordingly, in this edition, barring has been maintained with as much regularity as seems consistent with the style of the music. When individual voice-parts go their own way rhythmically (as they often do) no attempt has been made to mark the music with accents, since these invariably correspond to natural stresses of the verse or of the words themselves. If each poem is read carefully before rehearsal begins, there should be no difficulty in sustaining natural verbal accents at all times and in all voice-parts. For similar reasons, normal tied notes have been preferred to archaic practices involving dots placed to the right of bar-lines. It should not be necessary in this day and age to remind performers that bar-lines do not always coincide with stress or accent. When there is a clear metrical change, however, the nature and extent of this is indicated in order to distinguish between a mensural shift (Byrd, *This sweet and merry month,* bars 27/28) and one that appears as a result of textual accents (Farmer, *A little pretty bonny lass,* bars 17/18).

Texts have been modernized and punctuated in order to assist interpreters in every possible way, for notwithstanding the variable qualities of English madrigal poetry, the sense of the composition as a whole should emerge clearly in any performance worthy of the name. Capital letters are used to indicate the beginning of a new line in the original poem, since very frequently composers take liberties in setting verse and consequently obscure the underlying structure.

A new feature of this edition will, it is hoped, improve at one and the same time clarity in harmony, declamation, and form. The early part of this introduction hinted at the generally casual attitude towards refinements in both composition and proof-reading as practised in Elizabethan times, and since so many important characteristics of the madrigal are adversely affected by cavalier treatment of this kind, an attempt has been made to incorporate as an editorial method a consistent plan which the present writer has used with success over a number of years.

The first principle is to ensure that musical homophony is matched where appropriate by verbal homophony, all voice-parts singing the same syllables more or less exactly aligned. The more sensitive composers seek this effect as a matter of course, changing the order of words where necessary in order to achieve clarity of declamation. In Bateson's *Down from above*, the third line of the poem begins 'She starts thereat', and this order of words is followed by soprano and bass. Alto and tenor, entering at a different point, reverse the order to 'Thereat she starts', which aligns the words without obscuring the sense:

Ex. 2

In Farnaby's *The curtain drawn*, there is an obvious pairing of voice-parts in bars 17–19 (in spite of the trio entry in bar 16) and the bass text has therefore been altered from the original and aligned to that of the tenor. Similarly, Morley's *Die now my heart* presents a muddled example of underlay in the original version at bars 90/91, but if the alto and tenor are brought into line with soprano and bass, the result is clear and unequivocal.

Another type of adjustment, minor in fact but major in its importance for ease of breathing and accuracy of ensemble, is the regularizing of cadences in so far as the length of their final chord is concerned. In this respect many composers are careful, but not sufficiently so for an entirely satisfactory solution to the problems raised. The original notation of bar 35 in Bennett's *O sleep, fond fancy* is as follows:

Ex. 3

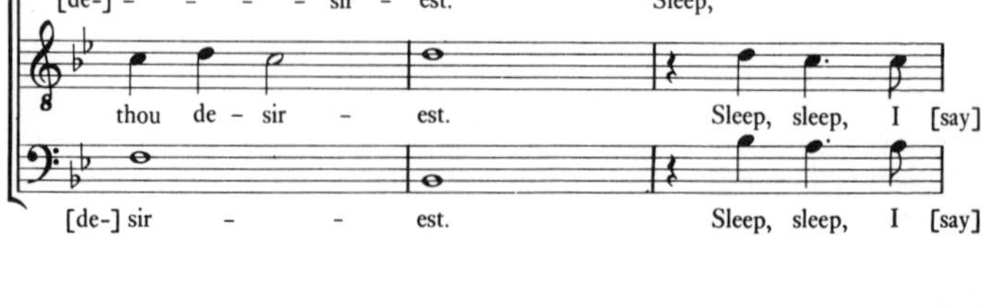

Soprano, tenor, and bass all hold their note to the end of the bar, since all have a rest of some sort before the beginning of the next phrase, 'Sleep, sleep, I say'; but the alto must begin this phrase on the very first beat of bar 36, and so his breathing space is neatly sliced from bar 35. This pragmatic approach nevertheless falls short of idealism, for three reasons. First, the rather audible ending 'st' of 'desirest' is heard twice in bar 35 – once when the alto finishes, and once again when the other three voice-parts finish. Second, when the alto stops singing, the spacing of the chord changes, and four-part harmony gives way suddenly to three-part. Third, the final 'st' of bar 35 is followed at once by a word whose opening sound is also sibilant, the aural effect being something like: 'desir*ests*leep'. One answer to the dilemma would be a pause on the bar-line. The solution adopted here, and at comparable points in other madrigals, is to standardize the length of the final chord, compromising between two beats in the alto and four beats in the other parts. All sing a dotted minim, which serves to bring the final 'st' in line and allow for a breath before the word 'Sleep'.

Occasionally a note has been clipped for harmonic reasons. There is a passage in Farnaby's *Construe my meaning* where a soprano note sustained for the written length would imply a discord in the second half of the bar:

Ex. 4

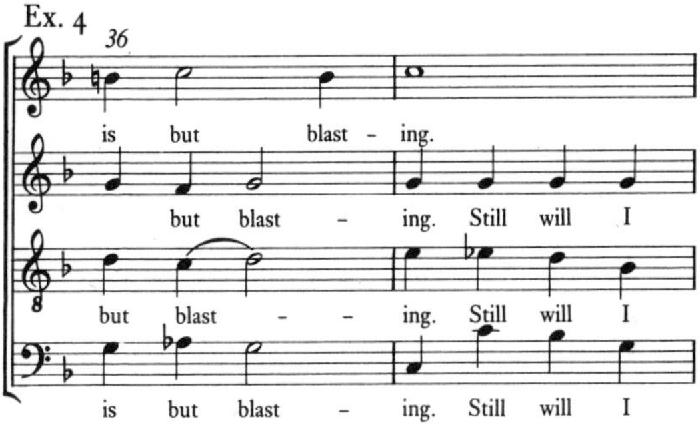

In the present edition, the soprano C has been changed to a minim. It could have been further trimmed to a crochet, but since the end vowel corresponds to that of the next word ('-ing / Still') there is no great harm done in leaving the C as a link between one phrase and another, the basic chord simply changing from major to minor. In Morley's *Say, gentle nymphs* we have an example of a sustained bass note which gives the effect of a momentary 6/4 chord; and later in the same madrigal a cadence in which three notes of a four-note chord (even when it changes position half-way through the bar) coincide on D.

Ex. 5

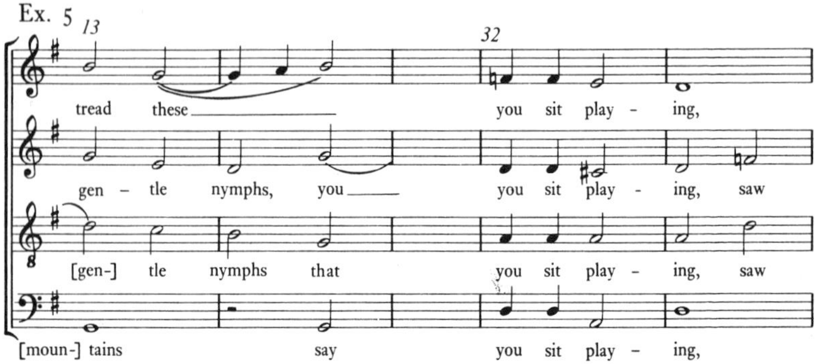

If the bass G in bar 13 is changed to a minim, the harmony reverts to normal; and when the soprano and bass D's are halved in bar 33, the alto-tenor entry sounds much clearer. On the other hand, it is not advisable to shorten the semibreve A's in bars 35 and 38 of the tenor part, since both places require that note for reasons of balance and fullness of sound.

It would be pedantic if every single instance of adjustment were made the occasion for a footnote, and in any event the prime purpose of this edition is a practical one. If performers feel that these editorial practices have been carried too far, all they have to do is to lengthen notes that feel uncomfortably short. But I do not think this very likely; and I have never experienced any objection from singers, who are only too willing as a rule to find new and artistic ways to unify breathing, phrasing, and declamation. To the members of my Ambrosian Consort (who have recorded some of these madrigals on HMV Mono HQM 1080 and Stereo HQS 1080) I extend my sincere thanks for many happy years of experiment and co-operation, and if the results as printed here add to the general pleasure of madrigal singing and eventually call for further volumes in this series, my hopes to extend and renew a most delectable form of vocal chamber music will not be in vain.

Columbia University DENIS STEVENS
In the City of New York
January 1966

I

DOWN FROM ABOVE

THOMAS BATESON

Down from above falls Jove in rain
Into fair Danaë's lap amain,
She starts thereat, yet lamblike still
At last performeth all his will.
Both high and low such golden gifts
Will put their conscience to the shift.

Madrigals I à 3, 4, 5, 6 (1604), ix
To those complaining of the shortness of most madrigals, answer should be given that a steady tempo helps matters amazingly. Bateson's witty setting of this fragment of Greek legend deserves to unravel itself at a leisurely pace, which may be fixed with reference to bar 12. The word 'still' in bars 18 and 20 implies quietness as well as immobility, so that the entire phrase could be sung softly. Danaë, of course, was the daughter of Acrisius, King of Argos. On hearing that she would bear a son destined to slay him, Acrisius shut her up in a chamber of stone or brass. Jove, disguised as a shower of gold, made her the mother of Perseus who grew up to manhood and fulfilled the prophecy by accidentally killing his grandfather with a discus.

- - nae's lap a - main, in - to fair Da -
fair Da - nae's lap a - main, in - to
In - to fair Da - nae's lap a - main, in -
In - to fair Da - nae's lap a - main,
10
- nae's lap a - main, in - to fair Da - nae's
fair Da - nae's lap a - main, in - to fair Da - nae's
- to fair Da - nae's lap a - main, in - to fair Da - -
in - to fair Da - nae's lap
15
lap a - main, She starts there - at, she starts
lap a - - main, There - at she
- nae's lap a - main, There - at she
a - - main, She
there - at, yet lamb - like still, yet lamb - like
starts, there - at, yet lamb - like still, yet lamb - like
starts, there - at, yet lamb - like still, lamb - like
starts there - at, yet lamb - like still, lamb - like

20
still, At last per - form - eth all his will,
still, At last per - form - eth all his will,
still, At last per - form - eth all his will, at
still, At last per -
25
at last per - form - eth all his
at last per - form - eth all his
last per - form - eth all his will, per - form - eth all his
- form - eth all his will, his
will. Both high and low such gold - en gifts, both high and
will. Both high and low such gold - en gifts, such gold - en
will. Both high and low such gold - en
will. Both
30
low such gold - en gifts, such gold - - - en
gifts, such gold - en gifts, such gold - - en
gifts, such gold - en gifts, such gold - en
high and low such gold - en gifts, such gold - en

35
gifts, Will put their con - science to the shift, will put their
gifts, Will put their con - science to the shift, will put their
gifts, Will put their con -
gifts, Will put their con - science
con - science to the shift, will put their con - science to the
con - science to the shift, will put their con-science to the
- science to the shift, will put their con - science
to the shift,
40
shift, will put their con - science to the
shift, will put their con - science to the
to the shift, will put their con - science to the
will put their con - science to the
shift, their con - science to the shift.
shift, their con - science to the shift.
shift, their con - science to the shift.
shift, their con - science to the shift.

2 IF LOVE BE BLIND

THOMAS BATESON

If Love be blind, how hath he then the sight
  With beauty's beams my careless heart to wound?
Or, if a boy, how hath he then the might
  The mightiest conquerors to bring to ground?
O no, he is not blind, but I that lead
  My thoughts the ways that bring to restless fears;
Nor yet a boy, but I, that live in dread
  Mixed with hope, and seek for joy in tears.

Madrigals I à 3, 4, 5, 6 (1604), xi
Note that only the accent, not the metre, must change between bars 7 and 13. A repeated phrase such as 'how hath he then the might' is useful in building to a climax, the crucial word being 'conquerors'. The sense of the final section lies in the contrast between Cupid and the poet-lover: Cupid is not blind, but I am – he is not a boy, but I am.

10
15
sight, With beau - ty's beams my care - less heart to wound, to
sight, With beau - ty's beams my care - less heart to wound, to
sight, With beau - ty's beams my care - less heart to wound, to
sight, With beau - ty's
wound, my care - less heart to wound, my care-less heart to
wound, my care - less heart to wound, my care - less heart to
wound, my care - less heart to
beams my care - less heart to wound, my care - less heart to
wound? Or, if a boy, or, if a boy, how hath he then the
wound? Or, if a boy, or, if a boy,
wound? Or, if a boy, how hath he then the
wound? Or, if a boy,
might, the might, how hath he then the might,
how hath he then the might, how
might, how hath he then the might, the
how hath he then the might, how

20
how hath he then the might
hath he then the might, the might
might, how hath he then the might,
hath he then the might, the might
The migh - tiest con - quer - ors to bring to ground, to
The migh - tiest con - quer - ors to bring to ground, to
The migh - tiest con - quer - ors to bring to ground, to
The migh - tiest con - quer - ors to bring to ground, the
25
bring to ground, the migh - tiest con - quer - ors to
bring to ground, the migh - tiest con - quer - ors to
bring to ground, the migh - tiest con - quer -
migh - tiest con - quer - ors to bring to ground, to
bring to ground?
bring to ground? O no, he is not
- ors to bring to ground? O no, he is not
bring to ground?

30
O no, he is not
blind, but I that lead, O no, he is not
blind, but I that lead
O no, he is not blind, but I that
blind, but I that lead My thoughts the
blind, but I that lead My thoughts the ways that bring to
My thoughts the ways that bring to rest - less
lead, but I that lead My
35
ways that bring to rest - less fears, that bring to rest - less
rest - less fears, my thoughts the ways that bring to rest - less
fears, my thoughts the ways that bring to rest - less
thoughts the ways that bring to rest - less fears;
40
fears; Nor yet a boy, but
fears; Nor yet a boy, but
fears; Nor yet a boy, nor yet a boy, but
Nor yet a boy, nor yet a boy, but

I, that live in dread, in
I, that live in dread, that live in
I, that live in dread, that live in
I, that live in dread
45
dread Mix - ed with hope, and
dread Mix - ed with hope, and
dread Mix - ed with hope, and seek for joy in
Mix - ed with hope, and seek for joy in
seek for joy in tears, mix - ed with hope, and seek for
seek for joy in tears, mix - ed with hope, and seek for
tears, for joy in tears, mix - ed with
tears, for joy in tears, and
50
joy in tears, for joy in tears.
joy in tears, for joy in tears.
hope, and seek for joy in tears.
seek for joy in tears.

3 PHYLLIS, FAREWELL

THOMAS BATESON

Phyllis, farewell, I may no longer live;
Yet if I die, fair Phyllis, I forgive.
I live too long; come, gentle death and end
My endless torment, or my grief amend.

Madrigals I à 3, 4, 5, 6 (1604), xii
Alfredo Obertello, in his valuable study of madrigal texts *(Madrigali Italiani in Inghilterra,* Milan, 1949) finds that this lyric has certain definite Italian features. The music, in contrast, has more affinity with the canzonet than with the madrigal, and the pervading touch of artless simplicity should be brought out in rehearsal and played down in performance. The phrase beginning on the last beat of bar 18 should be carried through bar 20/21 to maintain the sense. A quick breath can be taken after 'torment'.

10
yet if I die, fair Phyl - lis, I for -
yet if I die, fair Phyl - lis, I for -
if I die, fair Phyl - lis, I for -
die, yet if I die,
- give, fair Phyl - lis, I for - give. I live too
- give, fair Phyl - lis, I for - give. I live too
- give, fair Phyl - lis, I for - give. I live too
fair Phyl - lis, I for - give.
15
long, I live too long, come, gen - tle death and
long, I live too long, come, gen - tle death and
long, I live too long, come, gen - tle death and
I live too long, come, gen - tle death and
20
end, come gen - tle death and end My
end, come gen - tle death and end
end, come gen - tle death and end My end - less
end, My end - less

end - less tor - ment, or my grief a - mend, or my grief
My end - less tor - ment, or my
tor - ment, or my grief a - mend, my grief a -
tor - ment, or my grief a - mend;
25
a - mend; my
grief, my grief a - mend; my end - less tor - ment, or my
- mend; my end - less tor - ment, or my grief a -
my end - less tor - ment, or my grief a -
end - less tor - ment, or my grief
grief a - mend; my end - less tor - ment, or my grief
- mend; my end - less tor - ment, or my
- mend; my end - less tor - ment, or my grief
30
1.
2.
a - mend. I live too - mend.
a - mend. I live too - mend.
grief a - mend. I live too - mend.
a - mend. - mend.

4 WHITHER SO FAST?

THOMAS BATESON

Whither so fast? See how the kindly flowers
  Perfume the air, and all to make thee stay.
The climbing woodbind clipping all these bowers,
  Clips thee likewise for fear thou pass away.
  Fortune our friend, our foe will not gainsay.
Stay but awhile; Phoebe no tell-tale is,
She her Endymion, I'll my Phoebe kiss.

Madrigals I à 3, 4, 5, 6 (1604), vii
This is the first verse of a poem set in full by Pilkington in his *First Book of Songs or Airs* (1605), where the final couplet appears as a refrain in all three verses. The second verse, with some alterations, appears as a madrigal in Pilkington's first set (1613). Bateson's treatment of the pastoral is full of delicate pictorial touches, and may have been conceived as a tribute to Dowland, whose *Lachrymae* motto appears at the opening and at bar 28.

air, and all to make thee stay.
all to make to make thee stay. The
air, and all to make thee stay. The climb - ing
The climb - ing wood - bind
10
The climb - ing wood - bind clip - ping all these
climb - ing wood - bind clip - ping all these bowers, all these
wood - bind clip - ping all these bowers, clip - ping all these
clip - ping all these bowers, clip - ping all these
15
bowers, Clips thee like - wise, clips thee like - wise, for
bowers, Clips thee like - wise, clips thee like - wise,
bowers, Clips thee like - wise, clips thee like - wise, for
bowers, Clips thee like - wise,
fear thou pass a - way, for fear
for fear thou pass a - way, for
fear thou pass a - way, for
for

20
thou pass a way. For - tune our
fear thou pass a way. For - tune our
fear thou pass a - - way.
fear thou pass a - - way.
friend, For - tune our friend, our foe will not gain -
friend, For - tune our friend, our
For - tune our friend, our foe will not gain -
Our foe will not gain -
25
say, our foe will not gain - say.
foe will not gain - say, not gain - say. Stay
say, our foe will not gain - say. Stay
say, will not gain - - say.
30
Stay but a - - while; Phoe - be no
but a - while; but a - while; Phoe - be no
but a - while; Phoe - be no
Stay but a - while;

tell - tale is, She her En - dy - mion, I'll my
tell - tale is, She her En -
tell - tale is, She her En - dy - mion,
Phoe - be kiss,
- dy - mion, I'll my Phoe - be kiss, I'll
I'll my Phoe - be kiss, she her En -
She her En - dy - mion,
35
she her En - dy - mion,
my Phoe - be kiss, she her En - dy - mion,
- dy - mion, I'll my Phoe - be kiss, I
I'll my Phoe - be kiss, I
1
2
I'll my Phoe - be kiss. kiss.
I'll my Phoe - be kiss. Stay kiss.
will my Phoe - be kiss. Stay kiss.
will my Phoe - be kiss. kiss.

5 O SLEEP, FOND FANCY

JOHN BENNETT

O sleep, O sleep, fond fancy,
My head, alas, thou tirest,
With false delight of that which thou desirest.
Sleep, sleep, I say, fond fancy
And leave my thoughts molesting,
Thy master's head hath need of sleep and resting.

Madrigals à 4 (1599), xii
All voices share a middle-to-low tessitura contributing to a total effect of restraint and quietude, so that the opening and closing sections can be sung in a natural and unforced manner, tonally intense but dynamically fairly even. The middle section (bars 25-35) calls for a more animated approach, but this should not be allowed to intrude too much upon the prevailing atmosphere. Morley's setting of this text (in his *Plain and Easy Introduction*) may well have prompted Bennett's memorable and expressive version appearing only two years later.

- cy, fond fan - cy, O sleep, O
fan - cy, fond fan - cy,
fond fan - cy, fond fan - cy, O
fan - cy, fond fan - cy, O
10
sleep, fond fan - cy, O
O sleep, O sleep, O sleep, O
sleep, O sleep, O sleep, fond fan - cy, O sleep, O
sleep, O sleep, fond fan - - - cy, fond
15
sleep, O sleep, fond fan - - - - - cy,
sleep, fond fan - - - - - - - - cy,
sleep, fond fan - cy, O sleep, fond fan - cy, My
fan - - - - - - - - - - cy, My
My head, a - las,
My head, a - las, thou tir - est,
head, a - las, a - las, thou tir -
head, a - las, thou tir - est, my

20
— thou tir – est, my head, a – las,
my head, a - las, thou
- - est, thou tir - - - - - - -
— head, a - las, thou tir – est, thou
— thou tir – est, thou tir – est
tir - est, thou tir - est, thou tir - -
- est, thou tir - est With
tir - est, thou tir - est With
25
With false de - light of that which
- est With false de - light of that which
false de - light of that which thou de - sir - est, which
false de - light of that which thou de - sir - est,
30
thou de - sir - est, of that which thou de - sir - -
thou de - sir - est, with false de - light of that which thou de - sir - -
thou de - sir - est, of that which thou de -
with false de - light of that which thou de - sir - -

- est, of that, of that which thou de - sir - -
- est, of that, of that which thou de -
- sir - est, which thou de - sir - est, of that which
- est, of that, of that which thou de -
35
- - - est. Sleep, sleep, I
- - sir - est. Sleep, sleep, I
thou de sir - est. Sleep, sleep, I say, fond fan - -
- sir - - - est. Sleep, sleep, I say, fond fan - -
40
say, fond fan - - cy, sleep, sleep, I say, fond
say, fond fan - - - cy,
- cy, sleep, sleep, I say, fond fan - cy, fond
- cy, sleep, sleep, I say, fond fan - cy,
fan - - cy, And leave my
And leave my thoughts and leave my
fan - - cy, And leave my thoughts mo -
And leave my thoughts mo - lest - - -

45
thoughts mo - lest - ing, Thy mas - ter's head hath need of
thoughts mo - lest - ing,
- lest - - ing, Thy mas - ter's head hath
- ing, mo - lest - ing, Thy mas - ter's head hath need of
sleep and rest - - ing, hath need of sleep
Thy mas - ter's head hath need of sleep and rest -
need of sleep Thy mas - ter's head hath need of sleep
sleep and rest - - -
50
and rest - ing, hath need of
- ing, sleep and rest - ing, need of
and rest - ing, and rest - ing, need of
- ing, of rest - ing, need of
sleep and rest - - - - ing.
sleep and rest - ing.
sleep and rest - ing.
sleep and rest - - - - ing.

6 WEEP, O MINE EYES

JOHN BENNETT

Weep, O mine eyes, and cease not,
Alas, these your springtides, methinks, increase not.
O when, O when begin you
To swell so high that I may drown me in you?

Madrigals à 4 (1599), xiii
Faced with such a poem, Bennett could hardly avoid referring to the melody of Dowland's *Lachrymae*, yet the disarmingly passionate plea brings forth a setting whose sensitivity is characteristic of Bennett alone. As his admirer Ravenscroft said (preface to the *Brief Discourse)*: 'the very life of that passion, which the ditty sounded, is so truly expressed, as if he had measured it alone by his own soul, and invented no other harmony than his own sensible feeling in that affection did afford him'.

10
eyes, weep, O mine eyes, and cease
cease not weep, O mine eyes and cease
O mine eyes, weep, O mine eyes and cease
O mine eyes, weep and cease
15
not, A - las, these your spring
not, A - las, these your spring - tides a -
not, A - las, these your spring - tides,
not, and cease not, A - las,
20
tides a - las, these your
- las, these your spring - tides, me-thinks, in -
a - las, these your
these your spring - tides, in -
25
spring - tides, me - thinks, in - crease not.
- crease not, me - thinks, in - crease not.
spring - tides, me - thinks, in - crease not.
- crease not, me - thinks in - crease not.

30
O when, O when
O when, O when
O when, O when be-
O when, O when be-
35
be-gin you To swell so
be-gin you To swell so
-gin you To swell so high that I may
-gin you To swell so high that I may
high that I may drown me in you, that
high that I may drown me in you, that
drown, that I may drown me in you, that
drown me in you, that
40
I may drown me in you? you?
I may drown me in you? you?
I may drown me in you? you?
I may drown me in you? you?
1
2

7 YE RESTLESS THOUGHTS

JOHN BENNETT

Ye restless thoughts, that harbour discontent,
Cease your assaults, and let my heart lament,
And let my tongue have leave to tell my grief,
That she may pity, though not grant relief.
Pity would help, alas, what Love hath almost slain,
And salve the wound that festered this disdain.

Madrigals à 4 (1599), ix

Both music and text should be allowed to flow along naturally until the cadence at 'though not grant relief', where experiment will help to determine the best way of hinting at the full stop and fresh material in the final couplet. Both this and the previous poem were set by Wilbye in his *Madrigals I à 3, 4, 5, 6* of 1598.

10
- bour dis - con - tent, dis - con -
har - bour dis - con - tent, that har - bour dis -
dis - con - tent, that har - bour dis -
- tent, dis - con - tent, that har - bour
- tent, that har -
- con - tent, that har - bour dis - - - -
- con - tent, that har - bour dis - con - tent,
dis - con - tent, dis - - - - - - -
15
- bour dis - con - - - - tent,
- - - - con - - - - - - tent,
that har - bour dis - con - tent, Cease
- - - - con - - - - - - tent, Cease
20
Cease your as - saults and
Cease your as - saults, as - saults and
your as - saults, cease your as -
your as - saults, cease your as -

let my heart la – ment, and let my heart la –
let my heart la – ment, and let my heart la –
- saults and let my heart la – ment, and
- saults and let my heart la – ment, and
25
– ment, la – ment, And let my tongue
– – – – ment, la – ment, And let my tongue and
let my heart la – ment, And, let my
let my heart la – ment, And let my
30
have leave to tell my
let my tongue have leave to tell my
tongue have leave to tell my
tongue have leave to tell my
grief, That
grief, That she may pi – ty,
grief, That she may pi – ty, though not grant re –
grief, That she may pi – ty, though not grant re –

35
she may pi - ty, though not grant re - lief, that she may
though not grant re - lief, that she may
- - - lief, re - lief, that she may pi - ty though not
- lief, that she may pi - ty though not grant re -
40
pi - ty, though not grant re - lief.
pi - ty, though not grant re - lief. Pi - ty would help, a -
grant re - lief, re - lief. Pi - ty would help, a -
- lief, re - lief.
Pi - ty would help, a - las, what
- las, pi - ty would help, a - las, what
- las, what Love hath
Pi - ty would help, a - las, what
45
Love hath al - most slain, al -
Love hath al - most slain, what Love hath
al - most slain, what Love hath
Love hath al - most slain, what Love hath

50
- most slain, hath al - - most
al - most slain, hath al - most
al - most slain, hath al - most
al - most slain, what Love hath al - most
slain, And salve the wound that
slain, And salve the wound that fest - ered
slain, And salve the wound that fest - ered this
slain, And salve the wound that
55
fest - ered this dis - dain, this dis - - - - -
this dis - dain, dis -
dis - dain, this dis - - - - -
fest - ered this dis - dain, that fest - ered this dis -
60
- dain, that fest - ered this dis - dain.
- dain, that fest - ered this dis - - - dain.
- dain, that fest - ered this dis - dain.
- dain, that fest - ered this dis - dain.

8 THIS SWEET AND MERRY MONTH

WILLIAM BYRD

This sweet and merry month of May,
While nature wantons in her prime,
And birds do sing, and beasts do play
For pleasure of the joyful time,
I choose the first for holiday
And greet Eliza with a rhyme:
O beauteous Queen of second Troy,
Take well in worth a simple toy.

Italian Madrigals Englished (1590), viii
Psalms, Songs, and Sonnets (1611), ix

This poem has been attributed to Thomas Watson, compiler of the *Italian Madrigals Englished*, whose two purely native products were Byrd's settings for four and six voices of this obviously occasional piece. The four-part setting was later reprinted in Byrd's 1611 collection. It has been suggested that one or the other version was sung at Elvetham in 1591, when Lord Hertford entertained Queen Elizabeth, but the date of first publication suggests an earlier occasion for the actual première. Byrd demonstrates with masterly ease his complete understanding of the Italian vein, and care should be exercised to bring out the apt contrasts of mood and measure that place this musical gem so firmly in the memory. For reasons of range, alto and tenor voices have been exchanged between bars 68 and 73, so that some adjustments in timbre and weight of tone may prove necessary.

5
this sweet and
and mer - ry, mer - ry month of
mer - ry month of May,
month of May, this
mer - ry, mer - ry month of May, of
May, and
this sweet and
sweet and mer - ry, mer - ry month of
10
May, While na -
mer - ry, mer - ry month of May, While na -
mer - ry, mer - ry month of May, While na -
May, While
- ture wan - tons, wan - tons, wan -
- ture wan - tons, wan - tons, wan - tons in
- ture wan - tons, wan - tons in her
na - - ture wan - tons, wan - tons,

15
- tons in her prime,
her prime, And birds do sing,
prime, And birds do sing,
wan - tons in her prime, And
And birds do sing,
and birds do sing, do sing, do
and birds do sing, do sing, and birds do
birds do sing, and birds do sing,
20
and birds do sing, and beasts do
sing, do sing, and beasts do play,
sing, and beasts do play, do
and beasts do play, play, and
play, play, and beasts do
play, and beasts do play,
play, and beasts do play, do play,
beasts, and beasts do play, do

25
play, do play, and beasts do play, do play,
do play, and beasts do play, do play,
and beasts do play, do play, and
play, do play, and beasts do play, do
do play
do play, do play
beasts do play For plea - sure,
play, do play For plea - sure,
For plea - sure,
For plea - sure,
30
for plea - sure of the joy - ful time, the joy - ful
time, the joy - ful time, I choose the first,
time, the joy - ful time, I
time, the joy - ful time, I choose the first, I
35

I choose the first for hol - i - day, for
choose the first for hol - i - day, hol - i - day,
choose the first, the first for hol - i - day, for hol -
choose the first for hol - i - day, for
40
hol - - - i - day, And greet E - li -
for hol - - - i - day, for hol - i - day,
- i - day, for hol - i - day, And greet
hol - i - day, for hol - i - day,
- za with a rhyme, and
And greet E - li - za with a rhyme,
E - li - za, E - li - za with a
And greet E - li - za,
45
greet, and greet E - li - za, E -
and greet, and greet E - li - za, E -
rhyme, and greet E - li - za, E - li -
and greet, and greet E - li - za, E -

50
- li - - - za with a rhyme, with a rhyme,
- li - za with a rhyme,
- - za with a rhyme, with a rhyme,
- li - za with a rhyme,
with a rhyme, a rhyme: O, O
with a rhyme, a rhyme: O, O
with a rhyme: O, O
with a rhyme: O, O
55
beau - te - ous Queen, O
beau - te - ous Queen, O
beau - te - ous Queen, O beau -
beau - te - ous Queen, O beau - te - ous
60
beau - te - ous Queen of
beau - te - ous Queen of se -
- te - ous Queen of se - cond
Queen of se - cond Troy,

65
se - cond Troy, Take well in worth,
- cond Troy, of se - cond Troy, Take
Troy, of se - cond Troy, Take
of se - cond Troy, Take
take well in worth a sim - ple toy,
well in worth, take
well in worth, take well in worth a sim - ple toy,
well in worth, take well in worth a
70
take well in worth a sim - ple toy, a
well in worth a sim - ple toy,
a sim - ple toy, take well in worth a
sim - ple toy, take well in worth a sim - ple
75
sim - ple toy, a sim - ple toy, a sim - ple
a sim - ple
sim - ple toy, a sim - ple toy, a sim - ple
toy, a sim - ple toy,

toy, a sim - ple toy, a sim - -
toy, a sim - ple toy, take
toy, take well in worth
take well in worth a sim - ple toy, a
80
- ple a sim - ple, a sim - ple, a
well in worth a sim - ple, a sim - ple,
a sim - ple toy, take
sim - ple toy, a sim - ple, a sim - ple,
sim - ple toy, a sim - ple toy,
sim - ple toy, take well in worth a
well in worth a sim - ple toy, take well in
a sim - ple toy, take well in worth
85
1
2
a sim - - - - ple toy. toy.
sim - ple toy, a sim - ple toy, a sim - ple toy. toy.
worth a sim - ple toy, a sim - ple toy. toy.
a sim - ple toy, a sim - - - - - ple toy. toy.

9 A LITTLE PRETTY BONNY LASS

JOHN FARMER

A little pretty bonny lass was walking
  In midst of May before the sun gan rise.
I took her by the hand and fell to talking
  Of this and that, as best I could devise.
I swore I would, yet still she said I should not
Do what I would, and yet for all I could not.

Madrigals à 4 (1599), xiv

The speed is to some extent determined by the ability of the singers to deal with the tongue-twister in bars 35-37, *poco staccato*. Loss of clarity will effectively blunt the edge of the poet's coyly audacious wit.

10
rise; a lit - tle pret - ty bon - ny
rise; a lit - tle pret - ty bon - ny
'gan rise; a lit - tle pret - ty bon - ny
sun 'gan rise; a lit - tle pret - ty bon - ny
lass was walk - ing in midst of May be -
lass was walk - ing, was walk - ing in midst of May be -
lass was walk - ing in midst of May be -
lass was walk - ing in midst of May be -
15
- fore the sun 'gan rise; I took her by the
- fore the sun 'gan rise; I took her by the
- fore the sun 'gan rise; I took her by the
- fore the sun 'gan rise;
20
hand, I took her by the hand
hand, I took her by the hand and fell to
hand, I took her by the hand and fell to talk - ing to
I took her by the hand and fell to talk -

25
and fell to talk - ing Of this and that,
talk - ing, and fell to talk - ing Of this and that,
talk - ing, and fell to talk - ing Of this and
ing Of this and
of this and that, of this and that,
of this and that, of this and
that, of this and that, of this and
that, of this and that, of this and
30
as best I could de - - - - - vise.
that, as best I could de - - - - vise.
that, as best I could de - vise, I could de - vise. I
that, as best I could de - - - - - - vise. I
I swore I would, yet
I swore I would, yet
swore I would, I swore I would,
swore I would, I swore I would,

35
still she said I should not, yet
still she said I should not, yet
yet still she said I should not
yet still she said I should not
still she said I should not Do what I
still she said I should not Do what I
Do what I would,
Do what I would,
40
would, do what I would, and yet for all I could
would, do what I would, and yet for all I could
do what I would, and yet for all I could
do what I would, and yet for all I could
1
2
not, and yet for all I could not; not.
not, and yet for all I could not; not.
not, and yet for all I could not; I not.
not, and yet for all I could not; I not.

10 FAIR PHYLLIS

JOHN FARMER

Fair Phyllis I saw sitting all alone,
  Feeding her flock near to the mountain side.
The shepherds knew not whither she was gone
  But after her lover Amyntas hied.
Up and down he wandered whilst she was missing;
When he found her, O, then they fell a-kissing.

Madrigals à 4 (1599), XV
Farmer's original note-values are slightly unfair to the fair Phyllis, and the repeated opening phrase has therefore been modified to help both declamation and breathing.

10
shep - herds knew not, they knew not whi - ther she was
The shep - herds knew not, whi - ther she was
The shep - herds
The
gone,
gone, But
knew not, they knew not whi - ther she was gone,
shep - herds knew not whi - ther she was gone,
But af - ter her lov - er, her lov - er, but af - ter her
af ter her lov - er, her lov - er, but af - ter her
But af - ter her lov - er, her lov - er,
But af - ter her lov - er,
15
lov - er A - myn - tas hied.
lov - er A - myn - tas hied.
but af - ter her lov - er A - myn - tas hied. Up and down he
but af - ter her lov - er A - myn - tas hied. Up and

20
Up and down he wan - dered,
Up and down up and down he
wan - dered, up and down up and
down he wan - - - dered, he
up and down he wan - dered.
wan - dered, up and down he wan - -
down he wan - dered, up and down he
wan - - - - - dered,
25
up and down he wan - dered, up and down he
- dered, up and down he wan - dered, up and
wan - dered, up and down he wan - dered,
up and down
wan - dered, up and down he wan - - -
down he wan - - dered, he wan - -
up and down he wan - dered, up and down he wan - -
he wan - - - - -

30
-dered, whilst she was miss - ing; When
-dered, whilst she was miss - ing; When
-dered, whilst she was miss - ing; When
-dered, whilst she was miss - ing; When
he found her,
he found her, O, then they fell a -
he found her, O, then they fell a -
he found her, O, then they fell a -
35
O, then they fell a - kiss - ing, a - kiss - ing, O,
-kiss - ing, O, then they fell a - kiss - ing, a - kiss - ing, O,
-kiss - ing, O, then they fell a - kiss - ing, a - kiss - ing, O,
-kiss - ing, O, then they fell a - kiss - ing, a - kiss - ing, O,
40
1
2
then they fell a - kiss - ing; kiss - ing.
then they fell a - kiss - ing; kiss - ing.
then they fell a - kiss - ing; Up and down he kiss - ing.
then they fell a - kiss - ing; Up and kiss - ing.

11 TAKE TIME WHILE TIME DOTH LAST

JOHN FARMER

Take time while time doth last;
Mark how fair fadeth fast;
Beware if envy reign;
Take heed of proud disdain.
Hold fast now in thy youth;
Regard thy vowed truth;
Lest when thou waxeth old
Friends fail and love grows cold.

Madrigals à 4 (1599), xvi
Taking his cue from the pun on 'time', Farmer offers here a vocal equivalent of the hexachord fantasia, and in view of the speculative nature of the interdependent words and music, a firm and deliberate tempo should be adopted.

time while time doth last, take
while time doth last, take
doth last;
last, doth last, take
10
time while time doth last; Mark how fair
time while time doth last; Mark
Mark
time while time doth last;
15
fa - - - - - deth fast, mark how
how fair fa - deth fast, mark how
how fair fa - deth
Mark how fair fa - deth fast, mark
fair fa - - - - - - deth fast; Be -
fair fa - deth fast; Be -
fast; Be - ware,
how fair fa - deth fast; Be - ware,

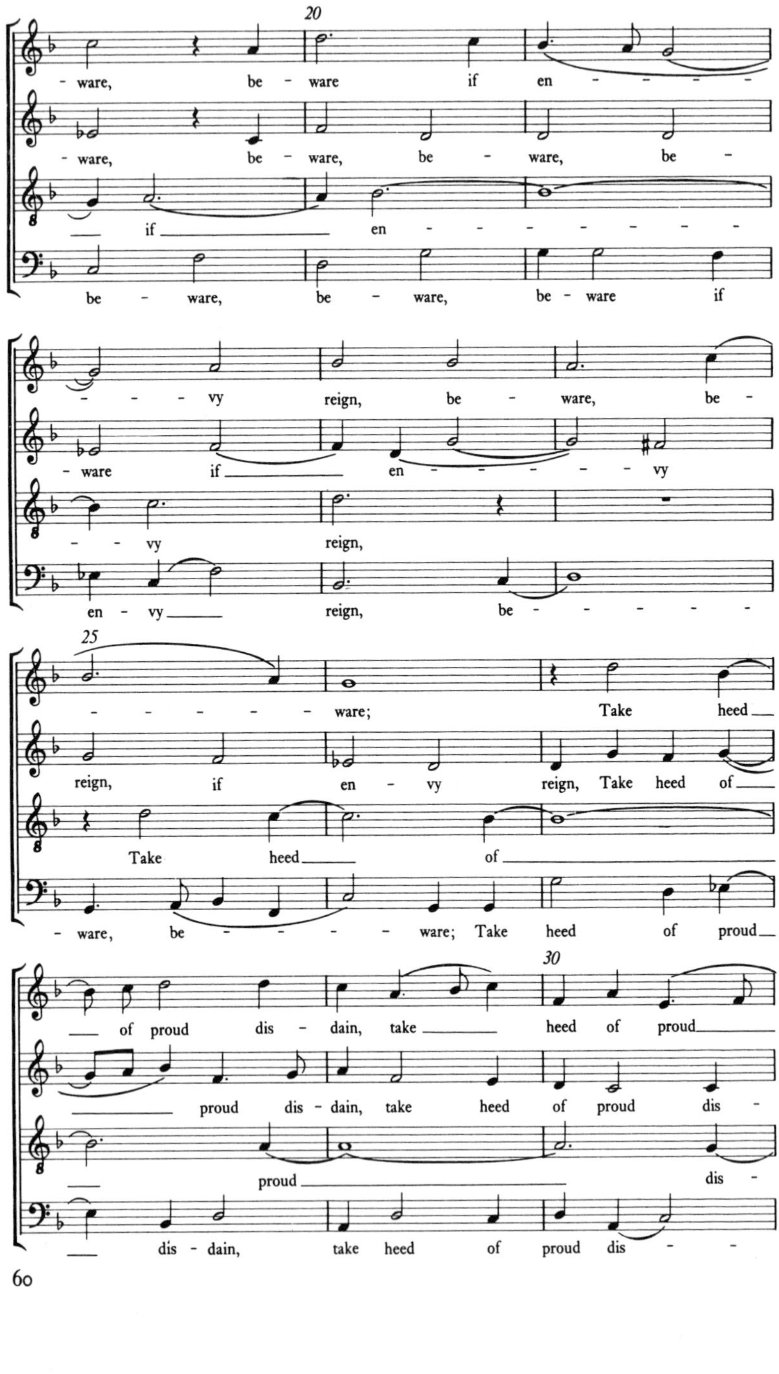

20
- ware, be - ware if en - - - - -
- ware, be - ware, be - ware, be -
if en - - - - - - - - -
be - ware, be - ware, be - ware if
- - - vy reign, be - ware, be -
- ware if en - - - - - vy
- - vy reign,
en - vy reign, be - - - - - -
25
- - - - - - ware; Take heed
reign, if en - vy reign, Take heed of
Take heed of
- ware, be - - - - - ware; Take heed of proud
30
of proud dis - dain, take heed of proud
proud dis - dain, take heed of proud dis -
proud dis -
dis - dain, take heed of proud dis - -

of proud dis - dain; Hold fast, now
- dain; of proud dis - dain; Hold fast,
- - - dain; Hold
- dain; take heed of proud dis - dain; Hold
35
in thy youth, now in thy youth,
now in thy youth, hold
fast, hold fast now in thy youth, hold
hold fast now in thy youth,
fast, hold fast now in thy
fast
fast, hold fast now in thy
40
hold fast, hold fast, hold fast now in thy
youth, in thy youth, hold fast now in thy
now
youth, hold fast, hold fast, hold fast now

45
youth, in thy youth,
youth, now in thy youth, now
in
in thy youth, thy youth, now in
now in thy youth, now in thy
in thy youth, in thy youth; Re-
thy youth;
thy youth, now in thy youth, now in thy
50
youth; Re-
gard, re-gard thy
Re-gard,
youth; Re-gard, re-
gard, re-gard, re-gard
vow-ed truth, re-gard-
thy vow-
gard, re-

55
thy vow - - - - - - ed truth; Lest when
thy vow - ed truth, thy vow - ed
- - - ed truth;
- - gard thy vow - ed truth, thy vow - ed truth; Lest
60
thou wax - - - - - - - - eth
truth; Lest when thou wax - - - - - - - - - - -
lest when thou
when thou wax - - - - - - - eth
old, lest when thou wax - - - - - - eth
- - - - - eth old, lest when
wax - - - - - - - - -
old, lest when thou, lest when thou wax - eth
65
old, thou wax - eth old, lest when thou wax - eth
thou wax - eth old, thou wax - eth old, lest when
- - - - - - - - - - - - - eth
old, thou wax - eth old, lest when thou wax - eth

old; Friends fail, friends
thou wax - eth old; Friends
old;
old; Friends fail, and love grow
70
fail and love grow
fail and love grow
Friends fail,
cold, friends fail and love grow
cold, and love grow cold, and
cold, and love grow cold, and love grow
and
cold, and love grow cold, and love grow
75
love grow cold.
cold.
love grow cold.
cold.

12 AY ME, POOR HEART!

GILES FARNABY

Ay me, poor heart!
Since Love hath played his part,
My senses are all lost,
My mind eke tossed
Like waves that swell.
Sweet god of Love,
Thou dost excel!
Thy passions move
My mind to prove
That turtle dove.
She flies; my love she tries.
Help, gods that sit on high!
O, send me remedy.

Canzonets à 4 (1598), xv
This is an adaptation of a song for solo soprano and three viols, and there is no harm done if some prominence is given to the uppermost line even in this madrigalian version. To avoid the threefold repetition of the same phrase in the alto between bars 51 and 54 the middle statement has been given to the soprano. Farnaby's own keyboard elaboration may be found in the *Fitzwilliam Virginal Book*, ii, 330.

Ay me, poor heart!
played his part, since Love hath played, hath
his part, since Love hath played his part,
his part, since Love
10
Since Love hath played
played his part, since Love hath played his part,
since Love hath played his part, since Love hath played his
hath played his part,
15
his part,
hath played his part, My sens - es all are lost, my
part, My sens - es all are lost, my sens - es
My sens - es all are lost, my
20
My sens - es all are lost, My
sens - es all are lost, My mind eke tossed, my
all are lost, all are lost, My mind eke tossed, my
sens - es all are lost, are lost, My mind

mind eke tossed
mind, my mind eke tossed Like
mind eke tossed Like waves that swell, like
eke tossed
25
Like
waves that swell, like waves that swell, like waves that
waves that swell, like waves that swell, like
Like waves that swell. Sweet
waves that swell.
swell. Sweet god of Love thou dost ex-
waves that swell, that swell. Sweet god of
god of Love, thou
30
Sweet god of Love, Thou dost ex-
-cel, sweet god of Love, Thou dost ex-cel! Thy
Love, thou dost ex-cel, sweet god of Love, thou dost ex-
dost ex-

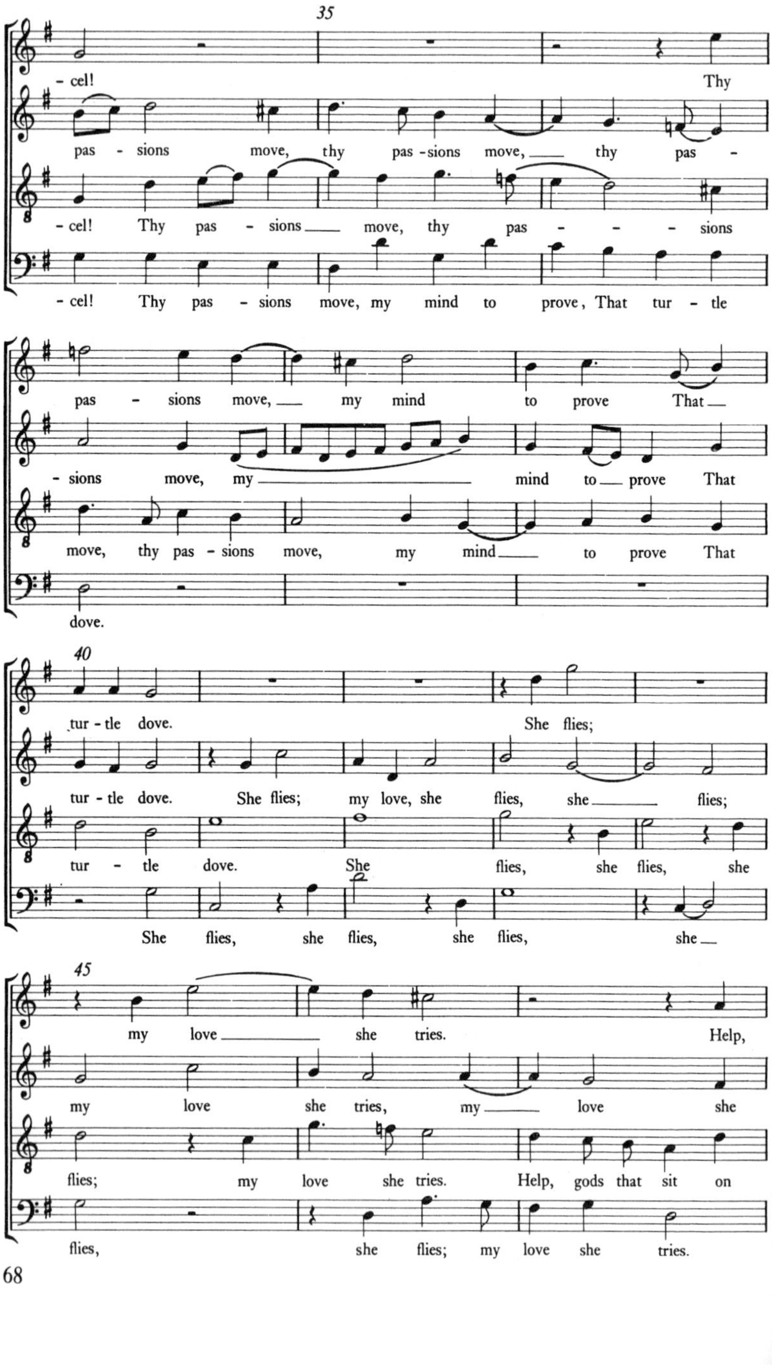
35
-cel! Thy
pas - sions move, thy pas - sions move, thy pas -
-cel! Thy pas - sions move, thy pas - - - sions
-cel! Thy pas - sions move, my mind to prove, That tur - tle
pas - sions move, my mind to prove That
- sions move, my mind to prove That
move, thy pas - sions move, my mind to prove That
dove.
40
tur - tle dove. She flies;
tur - tle dove. She flies; my love, she flies, she flies;
tur - tle dove. She flies, she flies, she
She flies, she flies, she flies, she
45
my love she tries. Help,
my love she tries, my love she
flies; my love she tries. Help, gods that sit on
flies, she flies; my love she tries.

50
gods that sit on high!
tries. Help, gods that sit on high! O send me re - me -
high, that sit on high! O send me re - me -
O send me re - me -
O send me re - me - dy,
- dy, O send me re - me -
- dy, O send me re - me - dy, send me re - me -
- dy, re - me - dy, O send me re - me -
55
O send me re - me - dy,
- dy, O send me re - me - dy, O send me re - me -
- dy, O send me re - me - dy, O send me re - me -
- dy, O send me re - me -
60
O send me re - me - dy.
- dy, O send me re - me - dy.
- dy, O send me re - me - dy.
- dy, O send me re - me - dy.

13 CONSTRUE MY MEANING

GILES FARNABY

Construe my meaning, wrest not my method;
Good will craves favour, witness the high God.
If I have meant well, good will reward me;
When I deserve ill, no man regard me.
What shall I say more? speech is but blasting.
Still will I hope for life everlasting.

Canzonets à 4 (1598), xx

Farnaby, who obtained an Oxford B.Mus. in 1592, seems not to have bothered over much with the more formal regulations of academic part-writing, but the odd soprano line in bars 17/18 may be the result of an attempt to avoid fifths between the soprano and tenor. They are however just avoided by the tenor's tied E. This faintly enigmatic text apparently tempted Farnaby into unusual realms of tonality, and special attention must be given to intonation and to the careful maintaining of pitch throughout.

10
me - - thod;
strue my mean - ing, wrest not
thod; Con - strue my mean - ing,
wrest not my me - thod, wrest not
15
Good will
my me - thod; Good will craves fa -
wrest not my me - thod; Good will craves fa -
my me - thod; Good
craves fa - vour, wit - ness the high
- - - - vour.
vour, wit - ness the high God, wit -
will craves fa - - vour, wit - ness the
20
God, the high God. If I have meant well,
If I have meant well, good will re -
- ness the high God. If I have meant
high God.

have meant well, if I have meant well, good
- ward, re - ward me, if I have meant well, good
well, meant well, if I have
if I have meant well, good
25
will re - - - ward me; When
will re - - ward me; When
meant well, good will re - ward me; When
will re - - ward me; When
30
I de - serve ill, no man re - gard, no
I de - serve ill, no man re - gard, me
I de - serve ill, no man re - gard
I de - serve ill, no man re -
man re - gard me. What shall I say more?
re - gard me. What shall I say more?
me. What shall I say more?
- gard me. What shall I say more?

35
what shall I say more, speech is but blast -
speech is but blast - - - ing, but blast -
speech is but blast - ing speech is but blast - -
speech is but blast - - - ing, but blast - -
ing. Still
ing. Still will I hope for life ev - er - last -
ing. Still will I hope for life ev - er - last -
ing. Still will I hope for life ev - er - last -
40
will I hope for life ev - er - - last - ing, for
ing, still will I hope for life ev - er - last - ing, I
ing, still will I hope for life, still will I hope for
ing, still will I hope for
life ev - er - last - ing.
hope for life ev - er - last - ing.
life, hope for life ev - er - last - - ing.
life ev - - er - last - - - ing.

14 SOMETIME SHE WOULD

GILES FARNABY

Sometime she would, and sometime not;
  The more request, the more disdained.
Each woman hath her gift, God wot,
  And ever had since Venus reigned.
Though Vulcan did to Venus yield,
I would have men to win the field.

Canzonets à 4 (1598), xvi

When the tenor voice moves into its uppermost register between bars 22 and 26, some difficulty may be experienced at first in maintaining an even balance, especially where the same figure occurs (at the same pitch) in the alto, as in bar 23. Careful rehearsal and listening will, in the end, improve matters; though the often angular nature of the tenor part must simply be negotiated as smoothly as possible. The references to Vulcan and his broad-minded wife are not without parallel in the music.

more dis - dained, the more re - quest, the
more re - quest, the more dis - dained,
some - time not; The more re - quest, the more dis - - -
and some - time not; The
10
more dis - dained.
the more re - quest, the more dis - dained, the
- dained, the more re - quest, the more dis - dained, the more dis -
more re - quest, the more dis - dained, the more re - quest, the
15
Each wo - man hath her gift, God
more dis - dained. Each wo - man hath her gift, God wot, each
- - dained. Each wo - man
more dis - dained.
wot,
wo - man hath her gift, God wot, each wo - man
hath, each wo - man hath her gift, God
Each wo - man hath her

hath her gift, her gift, God
wot, each wo - man hath her gift, God wot,
gift, God wot, her gift, God
20
And ev - er had since
wot, And ev - er had since Ve - nus reign - -
her gift, God wot,
wot, And ev - - - -
Ve - nus reign - - - - ed,
- ed, since Ve - nus reign - - ed,
And ev - er had since Ve - - - -
- - - er had, and
25
and
and ev - er had since Ve - nus
- nus reign - ed, and ev - er
ev - er had since Ve - nus reigned, Ve - nus

ev - er had since Ve - nus reign - ed,
reigned, and ev - er had
had since Ve - nus reigned, and
reigned, and ev - er had since Ve - -
and ev - er had since Ve - nus reigned, and
since Ve - - nus reign - ed,
ev - er had since Ve - nus reigned, ev - er had since
- nus reigned, ev
30
ev - er had since Ve - nus reigned.
and ev - er had since Ve - nus
Ve - nus reigned, ev - er had since Ve - nus
- er had since Ve - nus
Though Vul - can, though Vul - can, though Vul - can,
reigned. Though Vul - can, though Vul - can, though
reigned. Though Vul - can, though Vul -
reigned. Though Vul - can, though

35
though Vul - can, though Vul - can, though Vul - can
Vul - can, though Vul - can, though Vul - can,
- can, though Vul - can, though Vul - can did
Vul - can, though Vul - - - - can did
40
did to Ve - nus yield, did to Ve -
though Vul - can did to Ve - nus
to Ve - nus, to Ve - nus yield, did to Ve -
to Ve - - - nus
- nus yield, I would have
yield, I would have men to
- nus yield, I would have men
yield,
45
men to win the field.
win the field, men to win the field.
to win, men to win the field.
I would have men to win the field.

15 THE CURTAIN DRAWN

GILES FARNABY

The curtain drawn, I saw my love lie sleeping;
  Thrice happy was that peeping.
  For viewing her sweet lying
Preserves my life and keeps my soul from dying.
Of thousand joys, missing her, I had missed all,
Whose sight revives me more than ruby, pearl, and crystal.

Canzonets (1598), xi
The original underlay is suspicious at many points, and has here been changed to conform with a more natural association of words and music, notably at bars 11-13, 17, 20-24.

Thrice
saw my love, my love lie sleep -
love, I saw my love lie, love lie sleep - -
drawn I saw my love lie sleep - - -
hap - py was that peep - ing, thrice hap - py was
- ing; Thrice hap - py, thrice hap - py
- ing; Thrice hap - py was
- ing; Thrice hap - py
10
that peep - - ing.
was that peep - ing. For view - ing her sweet
that peep - - ing. For
was that peep - ing.
For view - ing her sweet ly - ing, her
ly - ing, view - ing her sweet ly - ing, for
view - ing her sweet ly - ing, for view - ing
For view - ing her sweet ly - ing,

15
sweet — ly - ing
— view - ing her sweet ly - ing Pre - serves my life, pre -
her sweet — ly - ing — Pre - serves my life and
ly - - - ing Pre - serves my life and
Pre - serves my life and keeps my soul from dy - ing, and
- serves my — life and — keeps my soul from dy - ing,
keeps, and keeps my soul from
keeps, and keeps my soul from
20
keeps my — soul from dy - ing. Of
and keeps my soul from dy - ing. Of thou - sand
dy - ing. Of thou - sand joys, miss - ing her,
dy - ing. Of thou - sand joys, miss - ing her,
25
thou - sand joys, miss - ing her, I had miss - ed all, Whose
joys, miss - ing her, I had miss - ed all, Whose
miss - ing her, miss - ing her, I had miss - ed all,
miss - ing her, I had miss - ed all,

sight re-vives me more, re - vives me more, whose
sight re-vives me more, whose sight re - vives me more, whose
Whose sight re - vives me more, me more,
Whose sight re - vives, re -
30
sight re - vives me more,
sight re - vives me more, re - vives me more, whose
whose sight re - vives me more, whose
- vives me more, whose sight re - vives me
whose sight re - vives me more, re-vives me
sight re - vives me more, whose sight re - vives me
sight re - vives me more than
more than ru - by, pearl,
35
more than ru - by, pearl, than ru - by, pearl, and crys - tal.
more than ru - by, pearl, than ru - by, pearl, and crys - tal.
ru - by, pearl, and crys - tal, ru - by, pearl, and crys - tal.
and crys - - - - tal.

16 APRIL IS IN MY MISTRESS' FACE

THOMAS MORLEY

April is in my mistress' face,
And July in her eyes hath place.
Within her bosom is September,
But in her heart a cold December.

Madrigals à 4 (1594), i
The word July should be stressed on the first syllable. Over-subtle attempts at vocal expression of the four seasons are clearly out of place in such a short and simple madrigal, yet a slight holding back on the melisma of 'September' and a more deliberate tempo (assisted by 'white' tone-colour) for the last line may serve to enhance the character of the performance as a whole. Morley probably took the idea from Vecchi's setting (1587) of Livio Celiano's poem *Nel vis'ha un vago Aprile,* where the first of nine verses presents a clear parallel.

10
in my mis - tress' face, And Ju - ly in her eyes hath
in my mis - tress' face, And Ju - ly in her eyes hath
face, my mis - tress' face,
face, my mis - tress' face,
place, And Ju - ly in her
place, And Ju - ly
And Ju - ly in her eyes hath
And Ju - ly in her eyes hath
15
eyes, her eyes hath place. With - in her bo -
in her eyes, her eyes hath place. With - in her bo -
place, her eyes hath place. With - in her bo -
place, her eyes hath place.
20
- som, with - in her bo - som is Sep - tem - - - - -
- som, with - in her bo - som is Sep - tem - - - -
- som, with - in her bo - som is Sep - tem - - - -
With - in her bo - som is Sep - tem - - - -

25
-ber, But in her heart, but in her heart, her
-ber, But in her heart, her
-ber, But in her heart, her heart,
-ber, But in her heart, but in her
30
heart, a cold De - cem - - - - - ber;
heart, a cold De - cem - - - - ber; But in her
a cold De - cem - - ber; But
heart, a cold De - cem - - ber;
But in her heart, but in her
heart, her heart, but in her
in her heart, but in her
But in her heart,
35
heart, her heart, a cold De - cem - - - - ber.
heart, her heart, a cold De - cem - - - ber.
heart, a cold De - cem - - ber.
but in her heart, a cold De - cem - ber.

17 DIE NOW, MY HEART

THOMAS MORLEY

Die now, my heart, from thy delight exiled,
Thy love is dead, and all our hope beguiled.
  O Death, unkind and cruel,
  To rob the world so
  Of that her fairest jewel!
Now shoot at me and spare not,
  Kill me, I care not!
O think not, Death, alas thy dart will pain me;
Why shouldst thou here against my will retain me?
  O hear a doleful wretch's crying,
  Or I die for want of dying.

Madrigals à 4 (1594), xix

Careful attention to declamation and timbre will be found to heighten the meaning of this brief but passionate threnody, which may even have been in the nature of an occasional composition. For once the play on 'dying', usually amatory if not downright erotic, occurs here in deadly earnest.

10
die now, my heart, from
- - - ed, from thy
- il - - - ed die now, my heart
die now, my heart, from thy de -
15
thy de - light ex - il - ed;
de - light ex - il - ed; Thy
from thy de - light ex - il - ed; Thy
- light, de - light ex - il - ed;
20
Thy love is dead, and all our hope be -
love is dead, and all our hope be - guil -
love is dead, and all our hope be - - -
25
- guil - - ed.
- - - ed, Thy love is dead, and all our
- guil - - - ed Thy love is dead and
Thy love is dead, and all our

30
O
hope be - guil - ed. O Death, thrice
all our hope be - - guil - -
hope be - guil - ed, our hope be - guil -
Death, O Death, un - kind and cru - el, un
cru - el, O Death, O Death, un -
- ed. O Death, O Death, un - kind, O Death, un -
- ed. O Death, O Death, un - kind and
35
- kind and cru - el, To rob
- kind and cru - el, To rob the
- kind and cru - el, To rob the world
cru - - el, To rob the world
40
the world so Of that her
world so Of that her fair - est jew - el,
so Of that her fair - est jew - - el, Of
so Of that her fair - est jew - el,

fair - est jew - - el, her fair - est jew -
Of that her fair - est jew - -
that her fair - est jew - el, jew - - el! Now
her fair - est jew - eł, her fair - est jew -
45
- el! Now shoot at me, now shoot and
- el! Now
shoot at me, now shoot and spare not, now
el! Now shoot at me, now shoot and
spare not, now shoot at me, now shoot and
shoot at me, now shoot and spare not, now
shoot at me and spare not, now
spare not, now shoot at me, now shoot and
50
spare not, now shoot at me and
shoot at me, now shoot and spare not, and spare
shoot at me and spare not, now shoot
spare, not now shoot at me and

60
65
spare not, Kill me, I care
and spare not, Kill me, I care
and spare not, Kill me, I care
spare not, Kill me, I care
not! O
not!
not! O think not, Death, a - las thy dart will pain
not! O think not, Death, a - las thy dart will
think not, Death, a - las thy dart will pain me;
O think not, Death, a - las thy dart will pain me;
me, think not thy
pain me, think not thy
Why shouldst, why shouldst thou here a - gainst my
Why shouldst, why shouldst thou here a -
dart will pain me; Why shouldst, why
dart will pain me; Why

70
75
80
will re - tain me, re - tain me?
- gainst my will re - tain me, gainst my will re - tain me?
shouldst thou here a - gainst my will re - tain me? O
shouldst, why shouldst thou here a - gainst my will re - tain me?
O hear a dole -
O hear
hear a dole - ful cry - - ing,
O hear a dole - ful, a
- ful, a dole - ful wret - ch's cry
a dole - ful wret - ch's cry - - -
here a dole - ful cry - ing, a dole - ful wret - ch's cry -
dole - ful wret - ch's cry - - -
- ing, Or I die for want of dy -
- ing, Or I die for want
- ing, Or I die for
- ing, Or I die for want

85
ing, or I die for want of dy -
of dy - ing, or I die, I die
want of dy - - - ing,
of dy - - ing, or I
90
ing, or I die for want of
or I die, die for want of
or I die for want for want of
die for want I die for want of
dy - ing, or I die,
dy - ing, I die for want, I
dy - ing, or I die for want, or I die for
dy - ing, or I die, I
95
I die for want of dy - ing.
die for want of dy - - - ing.
want, for want of dy - - ing.
die for want of dy - - - - ing.

18 NOW IS THE GENTLE SEASON; THE FIELDS ABROAD

THOMAS MORLEY

Now is the gentle season freshly flowering,
To sing and play and dance while May endureth;
And woo and wed, that sweet delight procureth.

The fields abroad with spangled flowers are gilded,
The meads are mantled, and closes;
In may each bush arrayed, and sweet wild roses.
The nightingale her bower hath gaily builded,
And full of kindly lust and love's inspiring,
'I love, I love,' she sings, hark, her mate desiring.

Madrigals à 4 (1594), ix-x

It would be a pity to force the tempo of this pleasant and leisurely pastoral: the requisite life and lightness should come from a springy phrasing closely allied to the sense of the words and the pulse of the music. A long pause between the two parts is not necessary, for the verse forms an entity even though the two musical halves offer distinct evidence of contrasted styles.

10
en - dur - - eth, while May en - dur - - -
- eth, while May en - dur - eth, to sing and play and
sing and play and dance while May, while May en - dur - -
To sing and play and
15
- eth, while May en - dur - eth,
dance while May en - dur - eth, to sing and play and
eth, while May en - dur - eth, to sing and play and dance while
dance while May en - dur - - eth,
to sing and play and dance while May en -
dance while May en - dur - eth, to sing and play and
May en - dur - eth, to sing and play and dance
to sing and play and
20
- dur - eth, while May en - dur - eth; And woo and wed
dance while May en - dur - - eth; And
while May en - dur - eth; And woo and wed
dance while May en - dur - - eth; And woo and wed

25
too, and woo and wed too, and
woo and wed too, and wed too,
too, and woo and wed too, and woo and
too, and woo and
woo and wed too, and woo and wed
and woo and wed too, and woo and wed
wed too, and woo and wed too, and
wed too,
30
too, and woo and wed, and woo and wed too, and
too, and woo and wed, and wed too, and
woo and wed too, and woo and wed, too, and
and woo and wed too, and wed too, and
35
woo and wed, that sweet de - light pro - cur - - - eth.
woo and wed, that sweet de - light pro - cur - eth.
woo and wed, that sweet de - light pro - cur - - - eth.
woo and wed, that sweet de - light pro - cur - - - eth.

40
The fields a - broad with spang - led flowers are
The fields a - broad with spang - led flowers
45
gild - ed, the
are gild - - - ed, with spang - led flowers
The fields a - broad with spang - led flowers are
The fields a - broad with spang -
fields a - broad with spang - led flowers are
are gild - ed, the fields with spang - led flowers
gild - - ed, the fields a - broad with spang - led
- led flowers
50
gild - ed, with spang - led flowers are gild -
are gild - ed, with spang - led flowers are
flowers are gild - - ed, with spang - led flowers are
the fields a - broad with spang - led flowers are

55
– – – ed, The meads are mant – led, the meads are
gild – ed, The meads are mant – led, the meads are
gild – ed, The meads are
gild – ed, The meads are
60
mant – led, the meads are mant – led,
mant – led, the meads are mant – led, the meads are
mant – led, the meads are mant – led, the meads are
mant – led, the meads are
the meads are mant – led, and clos – es; In
mant – led, the meads are mant – led, and clos – es;
mant – led, the meads are mant – led, and clos – es; In
mant – led, the meads are mant – led, and clos – es; In
65
may each bush ar – ray – ed, and sweet, and
In may each bush ar – ray – ed, and
may each bush ar – ray – ed, and
may each bush ar – ray – ed, and sweet wild

70
sweet wild ros - es, and sweet wild ros - es. The
sweet wild ros - es, and sweet wild ros - es.
sweet wild ros - es, and sweet wild ros - es.
ros - - - es, and sweet wild ros - es.
75
night - in - gale her bower hath gai - - -
The night - in - gale her bower hath gai - ly
The night - in - gale her bower hath gai - - ly,
80
- ly, build - ed, the night - in - gale her
build - ed, the night - in - gale her bower hath gai -
gai - ly build - ed, the night - in - gale her bower,
The night - in - gale her bower hath
bower hath gai - ly, hath gai - ly build - ed, And
- ly build - ed, hath gai - ly build - - ed, And
her bower hath gai - - ly, gai - ly build - ed, And
gai - ly, hath gai - ly build - - ed,

85
full of kind - ly lust, and love's in - spir - ing, 'I
full of kind - ly lust, and love's in - spir - ing, 'I
full of kind - ly lust, and love's in - spir - ing, 'I
and love's in - spir - ing, 'I
90
love, I love, I love, I love, I love, I love,' she
love, I love, I love, I love, I love, I love,' she
love, I love, I love, I love, I love, I love,' she
love, I love, I love, I love, I love, I love,' she
sings, hark: 'I love, I love,' she sings, hark: her
sings, hark: 'I love, I love,' she sings, hark: her
sings, hark: 'I love, I love,' she sings, hark: her
sings, hark: 'I love, I love,' she sings, hark: her
95
1
2
mate de - sir - - - ing; and - ing.
mate de - sir - - - - ing; and - ing.
mate de - sir - - - - - ing; and - ing.
mate de - sir - - - ing; - ing;

19 SAY, GENTLE NYMPHS

THOMAS MORLEY

Say, gentle nymphs that tread these mountains,
  Whilst sweetly you sit playing,
  Saw you my Daphne straying
Along your crystal fountains?
  If so you chance to meet her,
  Kiss her and kindly greet her.
Then these sweet garlands take her,
And say from me, I never will forsake her.

Madrigals à 4 (1594), xx

Some of Morley's poets use 'while' as a conjunction instead of 'whilst', and in view of this it might be permissible for the sake of euphony to change the beginning of line 2.

15
nymphs that tread these mountains, these
tle gentle nymphs you that tread these
gentle nymphs that tread these mountains,
mountains, say, gentle nymphs that tread these
20
mountains,
mountains, Whilst sweet-
tains, Whilst sweetly you sit play-
mountains, Whilst sweetly you sit play-
25
Whilst sweetly playing, whilst sweetly,
ly you sit playing, whilst sweet-ly, sweet-ly,
ing, you sit playing, whilst sweetly,
ing, sit playing, whilst
sweetly you sit playing, sit play-
sweet-ly you sit playing, you sit play-
you sit playing, whilst sweet-ly you sit play-
sweetly, sweet-ly you sit play-

30
- ing, sweet - ly sit play - ing, whilst sweet - ly
- ing, sweet - ly sit play - ing, whilst sweet - ly
- ing, sweet - ly sit play - ing, whilst sweet - ly
- ing, sweet - ly sit play - ing, whilst sweet - ly
35
you sit play - ing, Saw you my Daph -
you sit play - ing, Saw you my Daph - ne, saw
you sit play - ing, Saw you my Daph - ne,
you sit play - ing, Saw
- ne, saw you my Daph - ne,
you my Daph - ne, saw you my Daph - ne, saw
saw you my Daph - ne, saw
you my Daph - ne, saw you my Daph - ne, saw
40
my sweet Daph - ne stray - - ing A -
you my Daph - ne, stray - - ing A -
you my Daph - ne, stray - ing A - -
you my Daph - ne, stray - ing A - long your

45
- long your crys - tal foun - - tains?
- long your crys - tal foun - tains?
- long your crys - tal foun - tains?
crys - tal foun - - - tains? If so you
50
If so you
If so you chance to
If so you chance to meet her,
chance to meet her,
chance to meet her,
meet her, Kiss her, O, and kind - ly
Kiss her and kind - ly
Kiss her, and kind - ly greet
Kiss her and kind - ly greet
greet, kind - ly greet her. Then
greet her, Kiss her and
her, and greet her.

55
her. Then these sweet gar - lands take
these sweet gar - lands, these sweet gar - lands take
greet her. Then these sweet gar - lands take
Then these sweet gar - lands take
60
her, And say from me,
her, And say from me,
her, And say from me, and say from
her, And say from me, and say from
and say from me, I ne - ver will
I ne - ver will for -
me, I ne - ver will, I ne -
me, I ne - - ver will for -
65
1
2
for - sake her; her.
- sake, for - sake her; her.
- ver will for - sake her; her.
- sake her; If so you her.

20

MY PRIME OF YOUTH

JOHN MUNDY

My prime of youth is but a frost of cares,
My feast of joy is but a dish of pain,
My crop of corn is but a field of tares,
And all my goods is but vain hope of gain.
The day is past, and yet I saw no sun;
And now I live, and now my life is done.

In deep distress to live without delight,
Were such a life as few I think would crave.
In pangs and pains to languish day and night,
Were too too much for one poor soul to have.
If weal and woe will thus continue strife,
A gentle death were good to cut off such a life.

Songs and Psalms à 3, 4, 5 (1594), xvii–xviii

These two madrigals undoubtedly belong together, since the keys agree as well as the metre and rhyme-scheme of the verses. The first verse comes from a poem said to have been written by Chidiock Tichborne on the eve of his execution in 1586, when Anthony Babington and his fellow-conspirators were unpleasantly put to death for planning to assassinate Queen Elizabeth and others of her household. Alison and East also set the first verse to music, following it by a second verse different from the one used by Mundy.

10
cares, My feast of joy is but a dish of
cares, My feast of joy is but a dish of
cares, My feast of joy, my feast
cares, My feast of
15
pain, my feast of joy is but a dish of
pain, my feast of joy is but a dish of
of joy is but a dish of
joy is but a dish of
20
pain, My crop of corn is but a
pain, My crop of corn, My
pain, My crop of corn is but a field of
pain, My crop of corn is but a field
25
field of tares, but a field, a field of tares,
crop of corn is but a field of tares, And
tares, but a field of tares,
of tares, is but a field of tares,

all my goods is but vain
And all my goods is but vain
And all my goods is but vain hope of
30
And all my goods is but vain
hope of gain, and all my goods is but
hope of gain, is but vain
gain, and all my goods is but vain hope, is
35
hope of gain. The day
vain hope of gain. The day is past, and yet
hope of gain. The day is past, the
but vain hope of gain. The day is past,
40
is past, the day is past, and yet
I saw no sun, the day is past, and yet I
day is past, and yet I saw no
the day is past, and yet I saw

45
I saw no sun; And
saw no sun; And now I
sun, I saw no sun; And now I live, now I live,
no sun; And now I live, and
now I live, and now my life is done,
live, and now my life is done, and now
and now I live, and now my life is
now my life is done, and now I live, and
50
and now I live, I live, and
I live, and now my life is done, and
done, and now I live, and now my
now my life is done, and
55
now my life is done, my life is done.
now my life is done, my life is done.
life is done, now my life is done.
now my life is done.

In deep dis - tress to
In deep dis - tress to live with - out de -
60
In deep dis - tress to live with - out de -
live with - out de - light, in deep dis -
light, to live with - out de - light,
In
65
- light, Were
- tress to live with - out de - light,
in deep dis - tress, to live with - out de -
deep dis - tress to live with - out de -
such a life as few, as few
Were such a life as few, I
- light, Were such a life as
- light, Were such a life as few, I

70
I think would crave.
think would crave, as few I think would
few I think would crave, as few I think
think would crave, as few I
In pangs and pains to
crave, as few I
would crave.
think would crave. In pangs and
75
lan - guish day and night,
think would crave. In pangs and
In pangs and pains to lan - guish
pains to lan - guish day and night, to
80
in pangs and pains to lan - guish day and
pains to lan - guish day and night, and
day and night, day and
lan - guish day and night, day and

night, Were too too
night, Were too much for one poor
night, Were too too much for
night, Were too too much for
85
much for one poor soul to have.
soul one poor soul to have.
one poor soul to have.
one poor soul to have. If
If weal and woe will thus con - tin - ue
If weal
weal and woe will thus con -
90
strife, if
If weal and woe will
and woe will thus con - -
- tin - ue strife, if weal and

95
— weal ___ and woe will thus con - tin - ue
thus con tin ue strife,
- tin - ue strife, con - tin - ue strife, A
woe will thus con - tin - ue ___
strife, A gen - tle death were
A gen - tle death were ___ good to ___
gen - tle death were good to cut, to
___ strife,
100
good to cut off such a life, to cut off
___ cut off ___ such a life, a ___
cut off such a
A
such a ___ life,
life, a gen - tle death were
life, a gen - tle death were
gen - tle death were good to cut off such

105
a gen - tle death were
good to cut off such a life, a
good to cut off such a life, to
a life,
110
good to cut off such a life,
gen - tle death were good to cut off such
cut off such a life, a
a gen - tle death were
a gen - tle death were good, were good to
a life, a gen - tle death were
gen - tle death were good to
good to cut off
115
cut off such a life.
good to cut off such a life.
cut off such a life.
such a life.

21 AMYNTAS WITH HIS PHYLLIS FAIR

FRANCIS PILKINGTON

Amyntas with his Phyllis fair in height of summer's sun
Grazed arm in arm their snowy flock; and scorching heat to shun
Under a spreading elm sat down, where love's delightments done,
'Down dillie, down,' thus did they sing, 'there is no life like ours,
No heaven on earth to shepherd's cells, no bell to princely bowers.'

Madrigals and Pastorals I à 3, 4, 5 (1613), vii
Since Pilkington's poet had his tongue in cheek while penning this naughty satire, a corresponding attitude may be emulated in the musical performance, which should in any event sound light-hearted and extrovert. A slight drop in dynamic level for the words 'thus did they sing' may be found effective in both repeats of the final couplet.

A - myn - tas with his Phyl - lis fair, in height of
height of sum - - - mer's sun, of sum - mer's
in height of sum - mer's sun, in
in height of sum - mer's
10
sum - mer's sun, in height of sum - mer's sun, in
sun, in height of sum - mer's sun, in
height of sum - mer's sun, in height of sum - mer's
sun, in height of sum - mer's sun, in
15
height of sum - mer's sun Grazed arm in arm, grazed arm in
height of sum - mer's sun Grazed arm in arm, grazed arm in
sun of sum - mer's sun Grazed arm in arm, grazed arm in
height of sum - mer's sun Grazed arm in arm, grazed arm in
arm their snow - y flock;
arm their snow - y flock; and scorch - ing heat to
arm their snow - y flock; and scorch - ing heat to
arm their snow - y flock;

20
and scorch - ing heat, scorch - ing heat to
shun, and scorch - ing heat to shun
shun, and scorch - ing heat to
and scorch - ing heat to shun, to
25
shun Un - der a
Un - der a spread - ing elm sat down, where
shun Un - der a spread - ing elm sat down,
shun Un - der a spread - ing elm sat down,
spread - ing elm sat down,
love's de - light - ments done,
un - der a spread - ing
un - der a spread - ing elm sat down,
30
un - der a spread - ing elm sat down,
un - der a
elm sat down, where love's de -
where love's de - light - ments done,

where love's de -
spread - ing elm sat down, where love's de -
- light - ments done, where love's de -
where love's de - light - ments done, de -
35
- light - ments done, 'Down, down, down, down,
- light - ments done, 'Down, down, down, down,
- light - ments done,
- light - ments done, 'Down,
down, down, dil - lie down, dil - lie down,
down, down, dil - lie down,'
'Down, down,
down, down, dil - lie down, down, down,
40
down, dil - lie down,' thus did they
thus did they
down, dil - lie down,' thus did they
down, dil - lie down,' thus did they

45
sing, 'There is no life like ours, no life like
sing, 'There is no life like ours, no life like
sing, 'There is no life like ours, no life like
sing, 'There is no life like ours, no life like
50
ours, No heaven on earth to shep - herds'
ours, No heaven on
ours, No
ours, No heaven on earth, no
cells, to shep - herds' cells, to shep - herds' cells, No
earth to shep - herds' cells, No
heaven on earth to shep - herds' cells, No
heaven on earth to shep - herds' cells, No
55
1
2
hell to prince - ly bowers.' bowers.'
hell to prince - ly bowers.' bowers.'
hell to prince - - - ly bowers.' bowers.'
hell to prince - ly bowers.' bowers.'

22 HAVE I FOUND HER?

FRANCIS PILKINGTON

Have I found her? O rich finding!
  Goddess-like for to behold,
Her fair tresses seemly binding
  In a chain of pearl and gold.
Chain me, chain me, O most fair,
Chain me to thee with that hair.

Madrigals and Pastorals I à 3, 4, 5 (1613), xi
This poem was set again by Bateson in his 1618 publication. A fairly leisurely, relaxed tempo may be found most suitable for the proper projection of the verse and its thought; bars 15-17 should be tested for balance where the two middle voices change places.

have I found her? O rich
have I found her? O rich find - ing!
found her? have I found
have I found her? have I
10
find - ing! O rich find - ing! God-dess -
O rich find - ing!
her? O rich find - ing! God-dess -
found her? O rich find - ing! God-dess like for
- like for to be - hold, God - dess -
God - dess like for to be -
- like for to be - hold, for to be -
to be - hold,
- like for to be - hold, God - dess -
- hold, God - dess - like for to be -
- hold,
God - dess - like for to be - hold,

15
like for to be - hold, Her
- hold, for to be - hold, for to be -
God - dess - like for to be - hold, to be - hold,
God - dess - like for to be - hold, Her fair
20
fair tress - es seem - ly
- hold, Her
Her fair tress - es seem - ly
tress - es seem - ly bind - - - -
25
bind - ing, her fair tress - es
fair tress - es seem - ly bind - ing, seem -
bind - ing, seem - ly bind - - ing, seem - ly
- ing, bind - - - ing,
30
seem - ly bind - ing, her fair tress - es
- - ly bind - ing, her fair tress - es
bind - - ing, her fair tress - es
her fair tress - es

seem - ly bind - ing In a chain of
seem - ly bind - ing
seem - ly bind - ing In a
seem - ly bind - ing
35
pearl and gold, in a chain of pearl and
chain of pearl and gold, of pearl and
In a
gold, in a chain of pearl and
In a chain of pearl and gold, in a chain
gold, in a chain of pearl and gold,
chain of pearl and gold, in a chain of
40
gold, pearl and gold, in a chain of pearl and
of pearl and gold, in a
of pearl and gold, in a
pearl and gold, in a chain of pearl and gold,

45
gold, in a chain of gold, in a
chain of pearl and gold, in a chain of
chain of pearl and gold,
in a chain of pearl and
(♩=♩)
chain of pearl and gold. Chain me,
pearl, of pearl and gold. Chain me,
of pearl and gold. Chain me,
gold, of pearl and gold. Chain me,
50
chain me, O most fair, Chain me to
chain me, O most fair, Chain me to
chain me, O most fair, Chain me to
chain me, O most fair, Chain me to
55
1
2
thee with that hair. hair.
thee with that hair. hair.
thee with that hair. hair.
thee with that hair. hair.

23 PALAEMON AND HIS SYLVIA

FRANCIS PILKINGTON

Palaemon and his Sylvia forth must walk,
Of passions past and divers things to talk.
He sighs, she weeps, they kiss, and both complain,
And both of them would something utter fain.
But voice and words were to them both denied,
For they had nought to say that was not said.

Madrigals and Pastorals II à 3, 4, 5, 6 (1624), xi
The word 'sighs' introduces the customary rests, since the Italian word 'sospiri' had this secondary meaning, and English madrigalists were quick to take it over as part of their veiled vocabulary. Let the diction of the almost tongue-tied lovers make its natural effect wherever possible. Tenor and bass underlay have been slightly changed between bars 11 and 13.

walk, Of pas - - si - - ons, pas -
walk, Of pas - - si - - ons past,
walk, Of pas - - si - - ons
walk, Of pas - - si - - ons past, of pas -
10
- - si - - ons past, of pas - - si - ons past and
of pas - - si - - ons past and
past, of pas - - si - - ons past and
- - si - - ons past and di - vers things to
15
di - vers things to talk. He sighs, he
di - vers things to talk. He sighs, he
di - vers things to talk. He sighs, he
talk, things to talk. He sighs,
sighs, she weeps, they
sighs, she weeps, they
sighs, she, she weeps, they
he sighs, she weeps,

20
kiss, they kiss and both com - plain,
kiss, they kiss and both com - plain, they
kiss, they kiss and both com - plain, they
they
they kiss, they kiss and
kiss, they kiss and both
kiss, they kiss and both com - -
kiss, they kiss and both com - -
25
both com - plain, And both of them would
com - - plain, And both of them
- - - plain, And both of them would
- - - plain, And both of them
some - thing, some - thing ut - ter fain, would some - thing,
would some - thing, some - thing ut - ter fain,
some - thing, some - thing, some - thing ut - ter fain,
would some - thing, some - thing ut - ter fain, would

30
some - thing ut - ter fain, would some - thing, some - thing
would some - thing, some - thing, some - thing ut - ter,
would some - thing, some - thing ut - ter fain, would
some - thing ut - ter fain, would some - thing, some - thing
35
ut - ter fain. But voice and words
ut - - ter fain. But voice and words were
some - thing ut - ter fain. But voice and words were
ut - ter fain. But voice and words
were to them both de - - - nied, were to them both de -
to them both de - nied, were to them both de -
to them both de - nied, were
were to them both de -
40
- nied, were to them both de -
- nied, were to them both de - - -
to them both de - - - -
- nied, were to them both de - - - nied

45
-nied, For they had nought to say,
-nied, For they had nought to say, for they had
-nied, For they had nought to
For they had nought to say,
say, for they had
nought to say, for they had nought to say that was not
say, for they had nought to say that was not
for they had nought to say that was not
50
nought to say that was not
said, that was not said, that
said, was not said, that
said, that was not said, that was not
1
2
said, that was not said. But said.
was not said, that was not said. But said.
was not said, was not said. But said.
said, that was not said. But said.

24 WHAT THOUGH HER FROWNS?

FRANCIS PILKINGTON

What though her frowns and hard entreaties kill?
I will not cease to love, affect her still.
Still will I love her beauty, hate her scorn,
Love her for beauty at her beauty's morn.

Madrigals and Pastorals I à 3, 4, 5 (1613), xii
The text suggests a clear scheme of dynamic levels, but it is important not to over-emphasize them at the expense of the shape of the work as a whole.

10
— en - trea - ties kill? what though her
— en - trea - ties kill? what though her frowns
— en - trea - ties kill? what though her frowns, what though her
what though her frowns, what though her
15
frowns and hard en - trea - ties kill? I
and hard en - trea - ties kill?
frowns and hard en - trea - - ties kill?
frowns and hard en - trea - ties kill?
20
will not cease to love,
I will not cease to
I will not cease to
I will not cease to love, I
I will not cease to love,
love, I will not cease to love,
love, I will not cease to
will not cease to love, I will not

25
I will not cease to love, I will not
I will not cease to love,
love, I will not cease to love,
cease to love, I will not
30
cease to love, af - fect her, af - fect her still.
I will not cease to love, af - fect her still.
cease to love, af - fect her, af - fect her still.
cease to love, af - fect her, af - fect her still.
Still will I love her beau - ty,
Still will I love her
Still will I love her beau - ty,
Still will
35
still will I love her beau - ty,
beau - ty, still will I love her
still will I love her beau - ty,
I love

still will I love her beau - ty,
beau - ty, still will I love her
Still will I love her beau - ty,
her beau - - - -
40
still will I love her beau - ty, hate her scorn,
beau - - ty, hate her scorn,
still will I love her beau - ty, hate her scorn,
- - - ty, hate her scorn,
Love her for beau - ty, Love her for beau - ty,
Love her for beau - ty, Love her for beau - ty,
Love her for beau - ty, Love her for beau - ty,
Love her for beau - ty, Love her for beau - ty,
45
at her beau - ty's morn, at her beau - - ty's
at her beau - ty's morn, at her beau - ty's

50
morn, at her beau - ty's morn,
morn, beau - ty's morn, at her
at her beau - ty's morn, at her beau - ty's
at her beau - ty's morn, at her beau - ty's
at her beau - ty's morn, at her
beau - ty's morn, at her beau - ty's morn,
morn, at her beau - ty's morn, at her beau -
morn, at her beau - ty's morn,
55
beau - ty's morn, at her beau - ty's morn, at her
at her beau - ty's morn,
- ty's morn, at her beau - ty's morn,
at her beau - ty's morn, at her
60
1
2
beau - ty's morn, her beau - ty's morn. morn.
at her beau - - - ty's morn. morn.
at her beau - ty's morn. morn.
beau - ty's morn, her beau - ty's morn. morn.

25 WHY SHOULD I GRIEVE?

FRANCIS PILKINGTON

Why should I grieve that she disdains my love,
  Or seek for love, since love's a grief?
A noble mind his tortures ill behove.
  He spoils, thralls, murders like a thief,
  Debarring beauty's bar all loved relief.

Madrigals and Pastorals I à 3, 4, 5 (1613), ix
A sustained opening and quiet singing will most effectively set the mood of this madrigal, whose poetical reference to 'debarring' prompts the observant Pilkington to a musical pun that should certainly be audible, even if invisible.

I grieve,
why should I grieve, why
grieve, why should I grieve,
grieve, why should I grieve, why
15
why should I grieve, why
should I grieve, why should I
why should I grieve, why should I
should I grieve, why should I
20
grieve, that she, that she dis-
grieve, that she dis-dains, that she dis-dains
grieve, that she dis-dains my love? that she dis-
grieve, that she dis-dains, that she dis-
25
-dains, dis-dains my love? Or seek for love,
my love? Or seek for love,
-dains, my love? Or
-dains my love? Or seek for love, or

30
or seek for love, or seek for
or seek for love, or seek for love, or
seek for love, or seek for love, or seek for love,
seek for love, or seek for love, or
love, or seek for love, since love's a grief?
seek for love, or seek for love,
or seek for love, since
seek for love, since love's a grief?
35
since love, since love's a grief, since love's a
since love's a grief, since love's a
love's a grief, since love's a grief, since love's a
since love's a grief, since love's a
40
grief? A no - ble mind, a
grief? A no - ble mind, a no - ble mind,
grief? A no - ble mind, a no - ble mind, a
grief? A no - ble mind, a no - ble mind, a

no - ble mind, a no - ble mind his
a no - ble, no - ble mind, a
no - ble mind, a no - ble, no - ble mind, a no - ble
no - ble mind, a no - ble mind, a no - ble mind
45
tor - tures ill be - hove, his tor - tures ill be - hove.
no - ble mind his tor - tures ill be - - hove. He
mind his tor - tures ill be - hove.
his tor - tures ill be - hove, his tor - tures ill be - hove.
50
He spoils, thralls, murd - ers like a
spoils, thralls, murd - ers like a thief, like
He spoils, thralls, murd - ers, he spoils, thralls,
He spoils, thralls, murd - ers like a
55
thief, he spoils, thralls, murd - ers like a thief,
a thief, he spoils, thralls, murd - ers
murd - ers, he spoils, thralls, murd - ers
thief, he spoils, thralls, murd - ers like a thief,

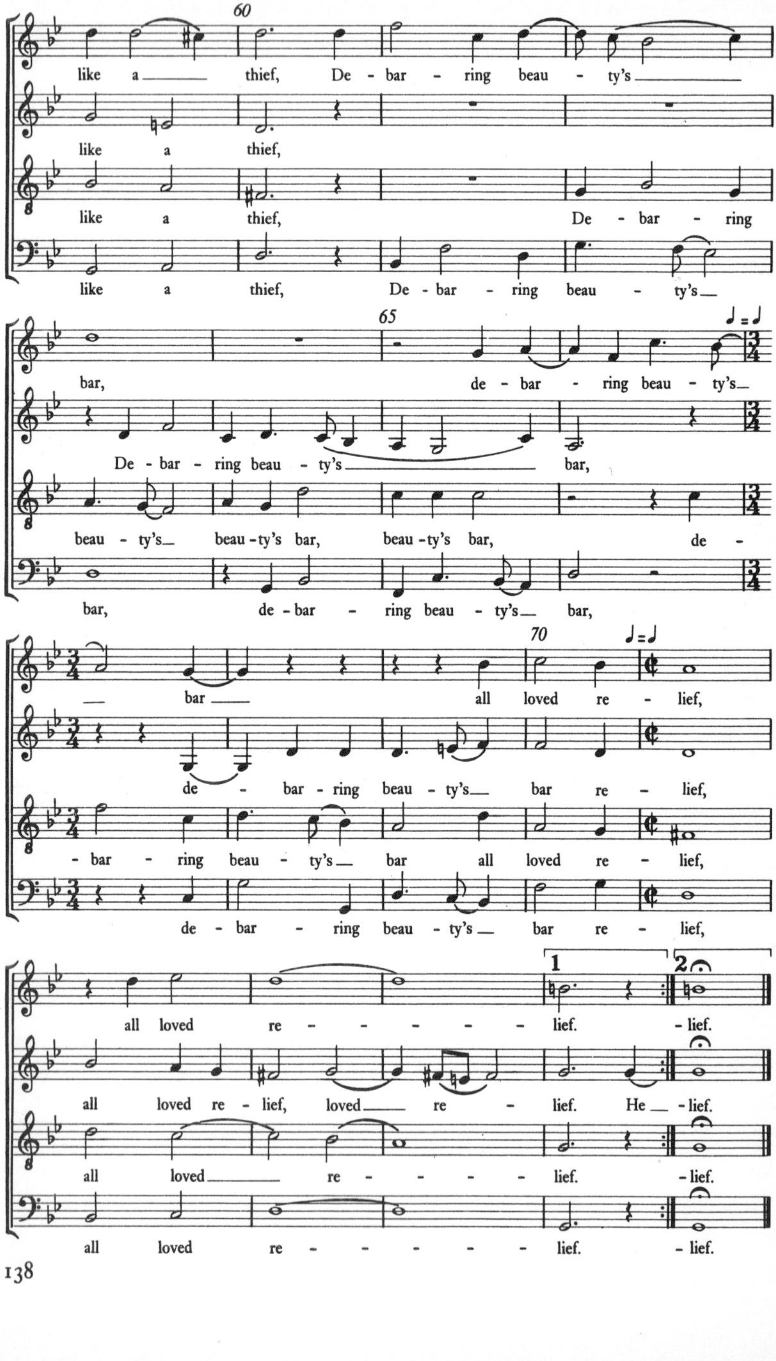
60
like a thief, De - bar - ring beau - ty's
like a thief,
like a thief, De - bar - ring
like a thief, De - bar - ring beau - ty's
65
bar, de - bar - ring beau - ty's
De - bar - ring beau - ty's bar,
beau - ty's beau - ty's bar, beau - ty's bar, de -
bar, de - bar - ring beau - ty's bar,
70
bar all loved re - lief,
de - bar - ring beau - ty's bar re - lief,
- bar - ring beau - ty's bar all loved re - lief,
de - bar - ring beau - ty's bar re - lief,
1
2
all loved re - lief. - lief.
all loved re - lief, loved re - lief. He - lief.
all loved re - lief. - lief.
all loved re - lief. - lief.

26 ADIEU, SWEET AMARYLLIS

JOHN WILBYE

Adieu, sweet Amaryllis,
For since to part your will is,
O heavy tiding,
Here is for me no biding.
Yet once again, ere that I part with you,
  Amaryllis, sweet, adieu.

Madrigals I à 3, 4, 5, 6 (1598), xii
Virgil's shepherdess has rarely appeared in so attractive a guise as here, and in spite of the obvious limitations in texture Wilbye has aimed at and achieved a most moving and memorable composition, which should be sung with due regard to key words and ideas. The change of key at bar 36 implies no hesitation in the rhythmic flow of the music.

a - dieu, a - dieu, a - dieu, sweet
- dieu, a - dieu, a - dieu, a - dieu, sweet
- ril - lis, a - dieu, a - dieu, sweet A - ma -
- dieu, a - dieu, a - dieu, sweet A - ma -
10
A - ma - ril - lis, For since to
A - ma - ril - lis, For since
- ril - - lis, For since to
- ril - - lis, For since
15
part, to part your will is,
to part, to part your will is,
part your will is,
to part your will is,
20
O hea - vy tid - - - -
O hea - vy tid - - ing,
O hea - - - - vy tid - - -
O hea - vy tid - - - - -

- ing, Here is for me no bid -
Here is for me, here is for me no bid -
- ing, Here is for me no bid -
- ing, Here is for me no bid -
25
- ing. Yet once a - gain, yet once a - gain, a -
- ing. Yet once a - gain, a - gain, ere
- ing. Yet once a - gain, yet once a - gain, a -
- ing. Yet once a - gain, a - gain, ere
30
- gain, ere that I part with you, yet
that I part with you,
- gain, ere that I part with you, yet once a -
that I part with you, yet
once a - gain, yet once a - gain, a - gain, ere that I
yet once a - gain, a - gain, ere that I
- gain, yet once a - gain, a - gain, ere that
once a - gain, a - gain, ere that I

35
part with you, A - ma - ril - lis,
part with you, A - ma - ril - lis,
I part with you, A - ma - ril - lis,
part with you, A - ma - ril - lis,
A - ma - ril - lis, sweet, a - dieu, a - dieu,
A - ma - ril - lis, sweet, a - dieu, a -
A - ma - ril - lis, sweet, a - dieu, a - dieu, a -
A - ma - ril - lis, sweet, a - dieu, a - dieu, a -
40
a - dieu; a - dieu, sweet A - ma - ril - lis,
- dieu, a - dieu; a - dieu, sweet A - ma - ril - lis,
- dieu, a - dieu; a - dieu, sweet A - ma - ril - lis,
- dieu, a - dieu; a - dieu, sweet A - ma - ril - lis,
45
A - ma ril - lis, sweet, a - dieu.
A - ma ril - lis, sweet, a - dieu.
A - ma - ril - lis, sweet, a - dieu, a - dieu.
A - ma - ril - lis, sweet, a - dieu, a - dieu.

27 AS MATCHLESS BEAUTY

JOHN WILBYE

As matchless beauty thee a phoenix proves,
Fair Leonilla, so thy sour-sweet loves.
For when young Acon's eye thy proud heart tames,
Thou diest in him, and livest in my flames.

Madrigals II à 3, 4, 5, 6 (1609), xv

According to one version of the legend of the phoenix, the eagle-like bird sought immolation on the funeral pyre at Heliopolis, a new young phoenix arising from the ashes. The poet's analogy with human love may be a little strained, but Wilbye takes full artistic advantage of what is offered. The suspensions and resolutions at 'sour-sweet loves' should be carefully planned and tuned.

- on - il - la, fair Le - - on - il -
Le - on - il - la; As
- il - - la, fair Le - on - il -
Fair Le - on - il - -
10
- la; As match - less beau - ty
match - less beau - ty thee a phoe - nix proves, Fair Le - on -
- la; As match - less beau - ty thee a phoe - nix
- la; As match - less beau - ty
15
thee a phoe - nix proves, Fair Le - on - il -
- il - la, fair Le - - on - il -
proves, a phoe - nix proves, Fair Le - on - il - -
thee a phoe - nix proves,
- la, so thy sour -
- la, Fair Le - - on - il - la, so thy sour
- la, Fair Le - on - il - la,
Fair Le - on - il - - la, so thy

20
- sweet loves, so thy sour - sweet
- sweet loves, so thy sour - - sweet
So thy sour - - sweet
sour - sweet loves.
25
loves. For when young A - con's eye thy
loves. For when young A - - con's eye thy
loves. For when young A - con's eye thy proud heart
proud heart tames, for when young A - con's
30
proud heart tames, for when young A - con's eye, thy proud heart
tames, thy proud heart tames, for
For when young A - con's eye
eye for when young A - con's eye, thy proud heart
tames, for when young A - con's eye thy proud heart
when young A - con's eye thy proud heart
thy proud heart

35
tames, Thou diest in
tames, Thou di - est in
tames, Thou diest in him,
tames,
40
him, and liv - - est in my
him, and liv - est in my
and liv - - est in my
flames, thou di - est in
flames, thou di - est in him,
flames, thou diest in
Thou diest in him
45
him; and liv - est in my
and liv - est in my
him; and liv - - est in my
and liv - - est in

50
flames; For when young A - - con's eye thy
flames; For when young A - con's eye thy
flames; For when young A - con's eye thy proud heart
my flames;
proud heart tames, for when young A - con's eye thy proud heart
proud heart tames, for when young A - con's
tames, thy proud heart tames, for
For when young A - con's eye
55
tames, for when young A - con's eye thy proud heart
eye for when young A - con's eye thy proud heart
when young A - con's eye thy proud heart
thy proud heart
tames, Thou di - est in
tames, Thou diest in
tames, Thou diest in him,
tames,

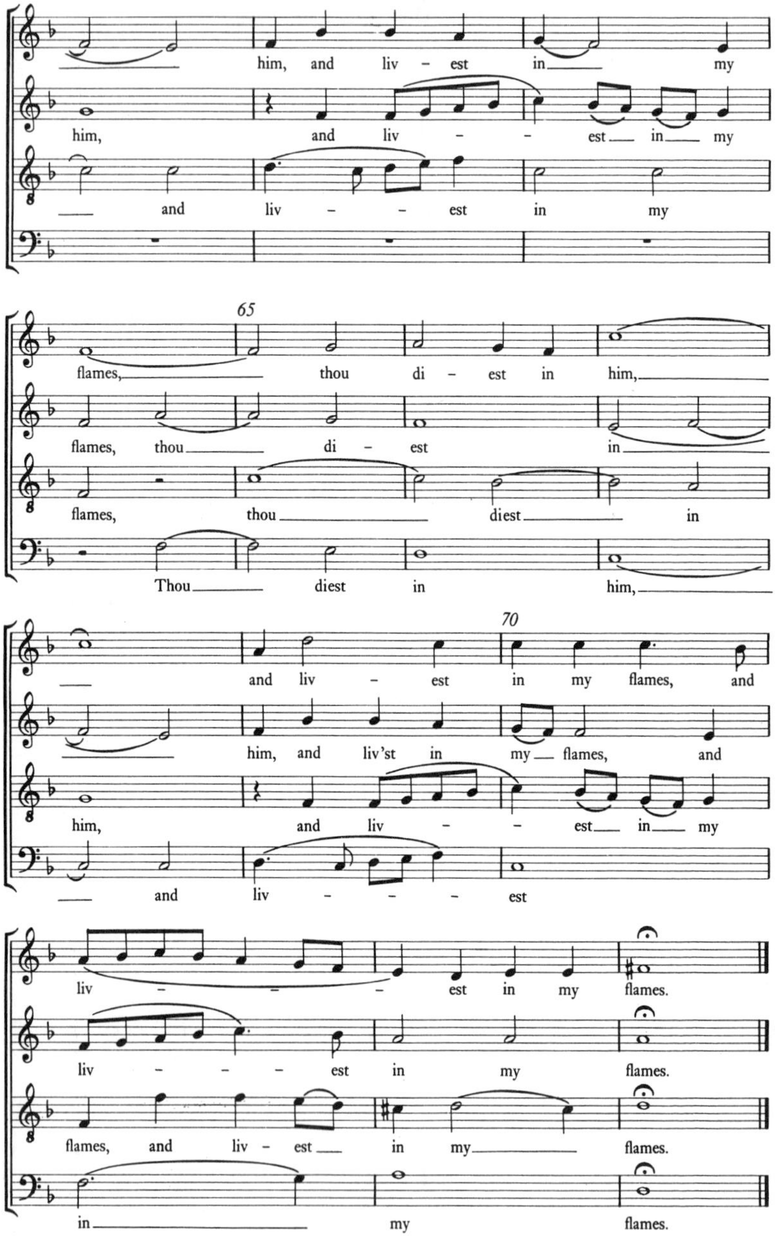
him, and liv - est in my
him, and liv - - est in my
and liv - - est in my
65
flames, thou di - est in him,
flames, thou di - est in
flames, thou diest in
Thou diest in him,
70
and liv - est in my flames, and
him, and liv'st in my flames, and
him, and liv - - est in my
and liv - - - est
liv - - - est in my flames.
liv - - - est in my flames.
flames, and liv - est in my flames.
in my flames.

28 LADY, WHEN I BEHOLD THE ROSES

JOHN WILBYE

Lady, when I behold the roses sprouting,
  Which clad in damask mantles deck the arbours,
  And then behold your lips where sweet love harbours,
My eyes presents me with a double doubting.
For, viewing both alike, hardly my mind supposes
Whether the roses be your lips, or your lips the roses.

Madrigals I à 3, 4, 5, 6 (1598), x
The poem is a translation of Angelo Grillo's *Quand'io miro le rose,* set by Marenzio (Book VIII à 5) and others. Wilbye found it sufficiently attractive for a second setting (this time for six voices) in his 1598 book, and at least two more Elizabethan translations existed, one of them appearing in Farnaby's *Canzonets* of 1598. The singular verb after 'My eyes' is correct according to sixteenth-century usage, when a pair of eyes was considered a unit. Rests have been added to bars 1 and 6 to assist in breathing and also to preserve the broadly-flowing triple metre. The basic pulse should not change at bar 11. In the final repeat, the upper two voices ought really to exchange parts, but if this makes bars 48-49 too high for the alto there is an easy solution.

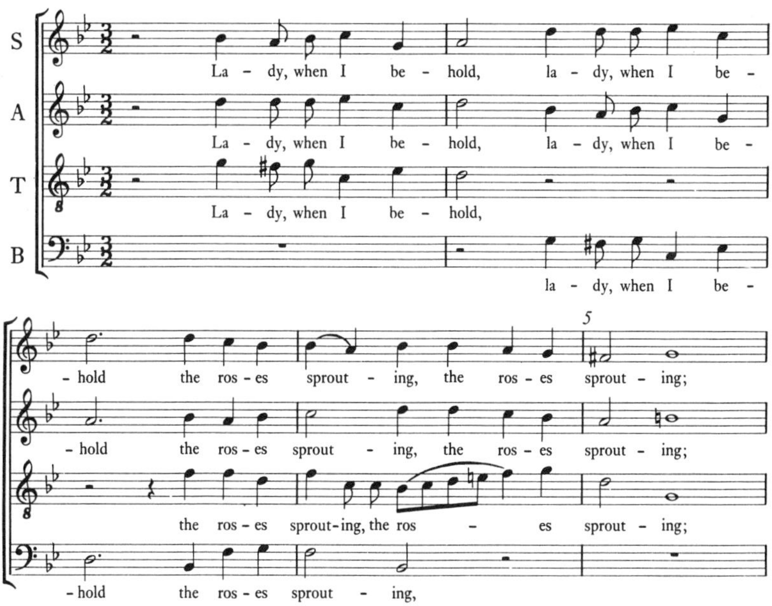

La - dy, when I be - hold, la - dy, when I be -
La - dy, when I be - hold, la - dy, when I be -
la - dy, when I be -
La - dy, when I be - hold,
10
- hold the ros - es sprout - ing, the ros - es sprout - ing, Which
- hold the ros - es sprout - ing, the ros - es sprout - ing, Which
- hold the ros - es sprout - ing, the ros - es sprout - ing, Which
the ros - - es sprout - ing, Which
clad in da - mask man - tles deck the ar - bours, which
clad in da - mask man - tles deck the ar - bours, which
clad in da - mask man - tles deck the ar - bours, which
clad in da - mask man - tles deck the ar - bours, which
15
clad in da - mask man - tles deck the ar - bours, And
clad in da - mask man - tles deck the ar - bours,
clad in da - mask man - tles deck the ar - bours, And
clad in da - mask man - tles deck the ar - bours,

20
then be - hold your lips, and then be - hold your
And then be - hold your lips, and then be -
then be - hold your lips, and then be - hold your
lips, and then be - hold your lips, where
hold your lips, and then be - hold your lips,
lips, and then be - hold your lips, where
25
sweet love har - - - bours, My eyes
where sweet love har - - bours, My
sweet love har - - - bours,
My eyes pre -
pre - sents me with a dou - ble, dou - ble doubt -
eyes pre - sents me with a dou - ble, dou - ble doubt -
My eyes pre - sents me with a dou - ble, dou - ble
- sents me with a dou - ble, dou - ble doubt - -

- ing, a dou - ble, dou - ble doubt - ing; My
- ing, a dou - ble, dou - ble doubt - ing; My eyes
doubt - ing, a dou - ble, dou - ble doubt - ing; My
- ing, My eyes pre -
35
eyes pre - sents me with a dou - ble, dou - ble doubt - ing.
pre - sents me with a dou - ble, dou - ble doubt - ing.
eyes pre - sents me with a dou - ble, dou - ble doubt - ing.
- sents me with a dou - ble dou - ble, doubt - - ing.
For, view - ing both a - like, hard - ly my
For, view - ing both a - like, hard -
For, view - ing both a - like, hard -
For, view - ing both a - like, hard -
40
mind sup - pos - - - es
- ly my mind sup - pos - es
- ly my mind sup - pos - es Whe - ther the
- ly my mind sup - pos - es

Whe - ther the ros - es
Whe - ther the ros - es
ros - es be your lips, or your
Whe - ther the ros - es be
45
be your lips, or your lips the ros - es
be your lips, or your lips the ros - es
lips the ros - - -
your lips,
whe - ther the ros - es
whe - ther the ros - es
- es whe ther the ros - es be your
whe - ther the ros - es be your
50
1
2
be your lips, or your lips the ros - es. - es.
be your lips, or your lips the ros - es. - es.
lips, or your lips the ros - es. - es.
lips, or your lips the ros - es. - es.

29 THUS SAITH MY CLORIS BRIGHT

JOHN WILBYE

Thus saith my Cloris bright
When we of love sit down and talk together:
'Beware of Love, dear,
Love is a walking sprite,
And Love is this and that,
And O I wot not what,
And comes and goes again, I wot not whither.'
No, no, these are but bugs to breed amazing,
For in her eyes I saw his torchlight blazing.

Madrigals I à 3, 4, 5, 6 (1598), xi
Wilbye here has recourse to a translation in *Musica Transalpina* (II, 21) of a madrigal by Marenzio, *Dice la mia bellissima Licori,* based on a poem attributed to Guarini. The mock seriousness of the girl's warning is perfectly mirrored in Wilbye's choice of texture, and deserves to be a feature of any really lively performance of this miniature masterpiece.

Thus saith my Clo - ris bright, When
we of love sit down and talk to - -
and talk to - ge - - ther,
talk to - ge - - ther, and
10
we of love sit down and talk to - -
- ge - - ther, and talk to -
Thus saith my Clo - ris bright, when we of love sit
talk to - ge - ther; Thus saith my
15
- ge - ther, and talk to - ge - ther;
- ge - ther; Thus saith my Clo - ris bright, when
down and talk to - ge - - ther; Thus
Clo - ris bright, when we of love sit down and
Thus saith my Clo - ris bright, when
we of love sit down and talk to - -
saith my Clo - ris bright, When we of
talk to - - ge - ther:

20
we of love sit down and talk to - ge -
- ge - - ther, and talk to - ge - -
love sit down and talk to - ge - -
and talk to - ge - -
- ther: 'Be - ware of Love, dear, Love is a walk - ing
- ther: 'Be - ware of Love, dear, Love
- ther: 'Be - ware 'Be - ware of Love, dear, Love
- ther: 'Be - ware of Love, dear, Love is a walk - ing
25
sprite, a walk - ing sprite,
is a walk - ing sprite, And love is this and that,
is a walk - ing sprite, And love is this and that,
sprite, a walk - ing sprite, And love is this and that,
30
And love is this and that, And O I
And love is this and that, And O I
And love is this and that, And O I
And love is this and that, And O I

35
wot not what, and O I wot not
wot not what, and O I wot not
wot not what, and O I wot not
wot not what, and O I wot not
what, And comes and goes a - gain, I wot not
what, And comes and goes a - gain, I wot not
what, And comes and goes a - gain, I
what, And comes and goes a - gain, I wot not
40
whi - ther, and comes and goes a - gain, I wot not
whi - ther, and comes and goes a - gain, I wot not
wot not whi - ther, and comes and goes a - gain, I
whi - ther, and comes and goes a - gain, I wot not
45
whi - ther.' No, no, these are but bugs to
whi - ther.' No, no, these are but bugs to
wot not whi - ther.'
whi - ther.' No, no, these are but bugs to

breed a - maz - - ing, No, no, these
breed a - maz - - ing,
No, no, these are but bugs to
breed a - maz - - ing, to
50
are but bugs to breed a - maz - - ing,
No, no, these are but bugs to breed a - maz -
breed a - maz - ing, to breed a - maz -
breed a - - maz - - ing,
For in her eyes
- ing, For in her
- ing, For in her eyes I saw
For in her eyes I saw his
55
I saw his torch - light blaz - - ing.
eyes I saw his torch - light blaz - ing.
his torch - - light blaz - ing.
torch - light blaz - - ing.